The New York Times

SUNDAY CROSSWORD PUZZLES
2009 ENGAGEMENT CALENDAR

Catalog No. D270
Published by Pomegranate Communications, Inc.
Box 808022, Petaluma CA 94975

Available in the UK and mainland Europe from Pomegranate Europe Ltd.
Unit 1, Heathcote Business Centre, Hurlbutt Road, Warwick, Warwickshire CV34 6TD, UK

Pomegranate also publishes *The New York Times Crossword Puzzles* 365-day tear-off calendar for 2009, along with more than 150 other calendars in wall, mini wall, engagement, specialty, and 365-day tear-off formats. In addition to calendars, products and publications in our extensive line include books, posters, postcards, books of postcards, boxed postcard sets, notecards, notecard folios, boxed notecard sets, magnets, mousepads, Knowledge Cards®, birthday books, journals, address books, jigsaw puzzles, designer gift wrap, stationery sets, and bookmarks. For more information or to place an order, please contact Pomegranate Communications, Inc., 800 227 1428, www.pomegranate.com.

Designed by Marshall Perin

Dates in color indicate US federal holidays.
Dates listed for all astronomical events in this calendar are based on Coordinated Universal Time (UTC), the worldwide system of civil timekeeping. UTC is essentially equivalent to Greenwich Mean Time. Moon phases and American, Canadian, and UK holidays are noted.

● NEW MOON   ☽ FIRST QUARTER   ○ FULL MOON   ☾ LAST QUARTER

2009

JANUARY

s	m	t	w	t	f	s
				1	2	3
4	5	6	7	8	9	10
11	12	13	14	15	16	17
18	19	20	21	22	23	24
25	26	27	28	29	30	31

FEBRUARY

s	m	t	w	t	f	s
1	2	3	4	5	6	7
8	9	10	11	12	13	14
15	16	17	18	19	20	21
22	23	24	25	26	27	28

MARCH

s	m	t	w	t	f	s
1	2	3	4	5	6	7
8	9	10	11	12	13	14
15	16	17	18	19	20	21
22	23	24	25	26	27	28
29	30	31				

APRIL

s	m	t	w	t	f	s
			1	2	3	4
5	6	7	8	9	10	11
12	13	14	15	16	17	18
19	20	21	22	23	24	25
26	27	28	29	30		

MAY

s	m	t	w	t	f	s
					1	2
3	4	5	6	7	8	9
10	11	12	13	14	15	16
17	18	19	20	21	22	23
24/31	25	26	27	28	29	30

JUNE

s	m	t	w	t	f	s
	1	2	3	4	5	6
7	8	9	10	11	12	13
14	15	16	17	18	19	20
21	22	23	24	25	26	27
28	29	30				

2009

JULY

s	m	t	w	t	f	s
			1	2	3	4
5	6	7	8	9	10	11
12	13	14	15	16	17	18
19	20	21	22	23	24	25
26	27	28	29	30	31	

AUGUST

s	m	t	w	t	f	s
						1
2	3	4	5	6	7	8
9	10	11	12	13	14	15
16	17	18	19	20	21	22
$^{23}/_{30}$	$^{24}/_{31}$	25	26	27	28	29

SEPTEMBER

s	m	t	w	t	f	s
		1	2	3	4	5
6	7	8	9	10	11	12
13	14	15	16	17	18	19
20	21	22	23	24	25	26
27	28	29	30			

OCTOBER

s	m	t	w	t	f	s
				1	2	3
4	5	6	7	8	9	10
11	12	13	14	15	16	17
18	19	20	21	22	23	24
25	26	27	28	29	30	31

NOVEMBER

s	m	t	w	t	f	s
1	2	3	4	5	6	7
8	9	10	11	12	13	14
15	16	17	18	19	20	21
22	23	24	25	26	27	28
29	30					

DECEMBER

s	m	t	w	t	f	s
		1	2	3	4	5
6	7	8	9	10	11	12
13	14	15	16	17	18	19
20	21	22	23	24	25	26
27	28	29	30	31		

1. SHUFFLING FEAT

BY FRANK LONGO / EDITED BY WILL SHORTZ / 06-05-05

ACROSS

1 See 115-Down
6 Not utopian
15 Obscures
19 "So long!"
20 Dickens orphan
21 "I'm working ___!"
22 Derived great pleasure from chastising?
24 Dream of Debussy
25 E-mail address component
26 Drink name suffix
27 More mad
29 Asks the Crocodile Hunter a series of questions?
37 Just so, after "to"
38 Itinerary stopover
39 Knock off
40 Broadway luminaries?
41 Dunces hurried up?
48 Unpaid debt
49 Winning
50 Irritation
53 Big inits. in overseas broadcasting
55 No nemesis
56 It might be found in a stall
59 Blockbuster, e.g., starts charging too much?
66 Massenet opera
67 Course goal
68 Rocky Mountain state: Abbr.
69 TV host Van Susteren
70 Weighing down Top 40 artists?
76 1983 Lionel Richie hit
77 They may clear the deck
78 Bing Crosby's "So ___"
79 Some hangings
80 Less than outstanding
84 Family men
89 Gets closer to a batch of hooch?
94 Right ___
97 1990's Ontario premier Bob ___
98 "Fire!" preceder
99 In ranks
100 Ditsy L.A. chick in intensive care?
107 Mexican muralist
108 Hamburger's one
109 Originally
110 Not sticking out
111 Postwar poets with camping wounds?
121 "And ___ bed"
122 Project without the band, perhaps
123 Some fancy hotel features
124 Schedule space
125 Lung problem
126 A layoff, unpolitely

DOWN

1 Noisy bird
2 Lit class reading
3 Bubkes
4 Aquatic shocker
5 Jacket material
6 Plum part
7 MapQuest request: Abbr.
8 Attorney or heir follower
9 Sword lilies, for short
10 Parcels
11 Starting cryptogram guess, perhaps
12 Bill's title buddy of film
13 With 93-Down, star-crossed
14 Glasgow's river
15 On the house
16 Painful combo
17 Yield
18 Rudderposts' places
20 Neighbor of Belarus
23 Palme ___ (prize at Cannes)
28 Is not on the street?
29 Anatomical canal
30 Come up to
31 Département head
32 Polit. designation
33 Starfleet Academy grad.
34 Level
35 Returning waves, of sorts
36 Saltimbocca ingredient
37 Fitness-advocating org.
42 New ___ (certain Nutmegger)
43 Suffix with smack
44 Anchor
45 Novelist McCaffrey
46 Woodworker's groove
47 Coaster with runners
50 Step face
51 Cords and barrels, e.g.
52 It's not the final release
54 Ancient emblems of royalty
55 Delivered
57 Beans
58 "King David" star, 1985
59 Exhaust, perhaps
60 Suggestions
61 Nickelodeon cartoon explorer
62 Mai ___
63 Somebodies
64 Inc. workers
65 Many a bust

Dec/Jan

66 Spanish tennis star Carlos
71 Clothes line
72 Undercover type
73 Kind of stick
74 Receptive
75 Thing, e.g.
81 More than a bit
82 Morales of movies
83 100 Cambodian sen
85 Spiced tea
86 Penn Station abbr.
87 Compound with double-bonded
   carbon atoms
88 Wrap (up)
89 Down-and-outer
90 Terminer's partner
91 Bad beginning?
92 Friction decreaser
93 See 13-Down
94 Princess Fiona in "Shrek," e.g.
95 Trifle
96 Greet, in a way
101 "What's Eating Gilbert Grape"
    director Hallström
102 Guarded
103 Karma
104 "Have ___ day!"
105 Response for passage
106 Suggest
112 Émile, par exemple
113 Climber's conquest
114 ___-i-noor diamond
115 With 1-Across, "Delilah" singer
116 It may be found under a top
117 Advanced degree?
118 Spleen
119 Sedona maker
120 Clinton's blown it

monday

29 ₃₆₄

---

tuesday

30 ₃₆₅

---

wednesday

31 ₃₆₆

NEW YEAR'S DAY   *thursday*

1 ₁

BANK HOLIDAY (SCOTLAND)   *friday*

2 ₂

---

saturday

3 ₃

---

s	m	t	w	t	f	s
				1	2	3
4	5	6	7	8	9	10
11	12	13	14	15	16	17
18	19	20	21	22	23	24
25	26	27	28	29	30	31

JANUARY

sunday

☽ 4 ₄

BY PATRICK MERRELL / EDITED BY WILL SHORTZ / 06-12-05

ACROSS

1 Pen filler
4 Unit of change
8 Sky line?
11 Calf accompanier
15 ___ Alto
16 Mexican silverworks city
17 Latino sports legend
18 Kind of infection, for short
19 "I ___ the opinion …"
20 Source of unrest
22 Flynn of film
23 Harem
25 Knock for a loop
26 Given the heave-ho
27 1-, 4-, 8- and 11-Across, when treated as 59-Across
33 Mideast land: Abbr.
34 Cowpoke's charge
35 Rubber
36 Company's plant, e.g.
40 They have hands and hooves
41 Michael Jackson movie musical, with "The"
42 Sir Henry for whom a gallery is named
43 Forty-niner's equipment
44 Tweet
46 Imbued with
48 Stub ___
49 They're adjacent to jibs
52 Formula One challenges
53 Splashdown recoveries
55 Baton Rouge sch.
56 Datum for a secy.
58 "___ the bat hath flown / His cloister'd flight …": Macbeth
59 43-, 44-, 80- and 81-Across, literally
63 Bygone carrier
66 With 9-Down, is compatible
67 Former press secretary Fleischer
68 Land-locked national
70 Ruhr Valley city
73 Ones higher up in a tree
76 Some
77 Out of stock
80 60's symbol
81 Puncture sound
82 Taking care of matters
83 Ultimate end
84 Peter, Paul or Mary
86 Substantial
87 With 103-Down, Shakespearean title character
89 Latin "earth"
90 Superfund administrator: Abbr.
92 112-, 113-, 114- and 115-Across (for this puzzle's theme)
99 Raised
100 Writer Bombeck
101 Standing
102 Biscayne Bay city
104 Rustic furniture material
107 Hot drink in a cup
108 Lombardy capital
109 Welk's "… and ___"
110 "Bellefleur" author
111 Mideast ruler
112 Big wheel site
113 Scale unit
114 Small fastener
115 General in the Capitol's Statuary Hall

DOWN

1 Animal with three lids on each eye
2 Prayer starter
3 Skim
4 More conniving
5 Mario Cuomo or Gray Davis, f'rinstance
6 Big maker of A.T.M.'s
7 ___ fault
8 Adjust, as an engine
9 See 66-Across
10 "So's ___ old lady!"
11 Cardiologist's exam
12 Mules
13 Business sect. listing
14 Org. with many goals
15 El ___
16 Agree (with)
17 Cajun French, e.g.
18 Battle of the ___
21 Churchill gesture
24 Heroic deed
26 Dazzle
28 "Do ___?"
29 Jazzes (up)
30 Friendly femme
31 Many a navel
32 Birdhouse dwellers
36 With some urgency
37 Lutelike instrument
38 Sweep
39 Just makes, with "out"
40 "To begin with …"
41 Oz. and kg.
44 B, basically
45 Work force that turns over a lot
46 Aspersion
47 Product with a circular red, white and blue logo

January

monday
5
5

tuesday
6
6

wednesday
7
7

thursday
8
8

friday
9
9

saturday
10
10

sunday
11
11

s	m	t	w	t	f	s
				1	2	3
4	5	6	7	8	9	10
11	12	13	14	15	16	17
18	19	20	21	22	23	24
25	26	27	28	29	30	31

3. NAME DROPPING

The New York Times

BY JOE BOWER / EDITED BY WILL SHORTZ / 06-19-05

ACROSS

1 One crossing a line
5 Major Libyan export
10 Checkers of entries, for short
14 Jock of 1970's-80's TV
19 It's the end of the world
20 Volunteer's words
21 Home of Interstate H1
22 School locator
23 The palest in the entire country?
26 Sauce with pine nuts
27 Pretty fast, on the highway
28 Checks a particular box
29 Big accident
31 Eur. smoker
32 Uncle Remus title
33 Front-end alignment
35 Live
36 Late conductor Sir Georg
37 Executive's golf score?
40 English quintet
42 Setting for an "Eloise" book
43 Coral reef dwellers
44 Down
47 Cover
50 Sign of success
51 "You don't say!"
53 2000 Democratic campaign slogan?
58 Plays a prank on, informally
61 Saddle attachment
62 [Ah, me]
63 ___ Hill, home of Theodore Roosevelt
65 Ingredient of a speedball
68 Gaming pioneer
71 After a while
72 There are lots of these for sale
74 Family nickname
76 Delete
77 Vote solicitor
78 Fashion trend featuring white suits and black ties?
83 Abbr. next to a telephone number
84 Goings on
85 Dirties
86 RR stop
87 Clash
90 Black who sang "Killin' Time"
92 Decorates expensively
95 Get a new boyfriend?
100 Detailed map
104 Horologist Terry
105 Drawn-out fight
106 Agitated state
107 Center of a square, maybe
108 Like some areas prone to flooding
110 Hidden valley
111 Extra
112 Turbine part
113 Comparable to a small child's R2-D2 toy?
117 Cubmaster, in Scouting
118 Film director Petri
119 Bluebloods
120 French peak
121 Villain
122 Sugary drinks
123 Chest material
124 Go like mad

DOWN

1 Jerks
2 Reawaken
3 Advanced British academic exam
4 Popular pistol
5 Orders
6 On vacation
7 Poetic contraction
8 "Get Shorty" novelist Leonard
9 Hit the ___
10 Hospital sights
11 One leaving its mark
12 "Caught you!"
13 Inspirations for many outdoor paintings
14 Neighbor of Francia
15 Torments
16 Toned
17 Untouched
18 Ones proceeding in the dark?
24 Navel type
25 New York ___
30 Early 11th-century year
32 Team that plays home games in Westwood
33 Clark who sang "Poor, Poor Pitiful Me"
34 Bouillabaisse ingredients
37 ___ Sci (college dept.)
38 Pizazz
39 County name in nine former Confederate states
41 "___ the Law" (Edward G. Robinson flick)
44 Breakfast container
45 Melodic passage
46 Former Toyota
48 1998 Sarah McLachlan hit
49 Army N.C.O.
51 Bowled over
52 On cloud nine

January

54 Somewhat
55 Alan of "Growing Pains"
56 "___ heavens"
57 Asian carrier, in brief
58 Sacred scrolls
59 Oktoberfest toast
60 One of the Finger Lakes
64 Montego or Grand Marquis, for short
66 Scottish refusals
67 Sea eagle
69 Beams
70 It's available at a "?" sign
73 "Hogan's Heroes" setting
75 Properly
79 City NE of Venice
80 D.C. group
81 "Would ___?"
82 Immigrant's class: Abbr.
83 U.P.S. driver's assignment
87 Kind of soup, in Southern cookery
88 Big oaf
89 Barnstormed
90 1990's White House occupant
91 Induction motor inventor
93 Airheaded
94 Sharply reproves
96 Off
97 Tom Clancy subj.
98 "Hold it!"
99 "Grand" thing
101 Patient's condition
102 Icy moon of Jupiter
103 Be on the brink
107 Dry
109 Cry from one using a hammer
110 Mustang competitors
111 So long
114 Past
115 "A pox on you!"
116 Preceder of 109-Down

monday

12 12

tuesday

13 13

wednesday

14 14

thursday

15 15

friday

16 16

saturday

17 17

s	m	t	w	t	f	s
				1	2	3
4	5	6	7	8	9	10
11	12	13	14	15	16	17
18	19	20	21	22	23	24
25	26	27	28	29	30	31

sunday

☾ **18** 18

JANUARY

4. HITTING THE SAUCE

BY MANNY NOSOWSKY / EDITED BY WILL SHORTZ / 06-26-05

ACROSS

1 Sci-fi carrier
9 Birds with green eggs
13 Like a record
20 Pasta ingredient
21 At sea
22 Strong and proud
23 Brewer's container
24 Saucy political group of the 1840's and 50's?
26 Jazz pianist Jarrett
28 Per ___ (how budgets may be planned)
29 Some football linemen: Abbr.
30 Classic saucy love song?
37 Sharp cheese
38 Cheep accommodations?
39 How anchovies are packed
40 Due
41 Be undecided
43 Without a shirt
47 Pal
48 Saucy health threat, according to the surgeon general?
53 "___ interested"
54 Choice on a multiple-choice test: Abbr.
55 Nods
56 Modern ice cream flavor
57 Unique
58 Carried away
59 Gulps down
61 Sustenance for Oliver Twist
62 Saucy yuletide plan?
68 Spaced out?
69 Muffle
70 Whom Jezebel worshiped
71 Rant and rave
72 Dover domestic
73 Ask (about)
75 Ranting and raving
78 It may be found in a pocket
79 Saucy payment system?
83 Guitarist Hendrix
84 Get scolded
86 Chicks follow them
87 Prancer's partner
88 ___ a beet
90 Mmes. of Madrid
92 Driveway surface
93 Had a saucy relationship?
97 Where clover grows
98 Ghostlike
99 One of the Seven Wise Men of ancient Greece
100 Saucy playground apparatus?
104 Go off
109 Riders
110 "Able was ___ ..."
111 Phone-answering instruction
112 Low wind instrument
113 ID's sought in phishing
114 Where William the Conqueror conquered

DOWN

1 Air France flier until '03
2 Ball-bearing item
3 Health standards org. since 1847
4 Sindbad hid behind its egg
5 Thirst-relieving
6 Cab Calloway's signature line
7 Frequent customer support locale nowadays
8 Cable for money
9 Little green man
10 Lamprey relatives
11 Online newsgroup system
12 Old British guns
13 Seize, slangily
14 El ___ (title for Juan Carlos)
15 Alley ___
16 Hot, in Vegas
17 Art appreciation
18 Middle-earth beings
19 TV actress Susan
25 Muslim mystic
27 Reddish hair dyes
30 Cook's drawer
31 Ann Landers was one
32 Drops
33 Word with turning or memory
34 Head lines, for short?
35 Man in a corner
36 "Gosh!"
41 Thin ice, e.g.
42 Copper head?
44 The blahs
45 Foot pads
46 Do
48 Restaurant option
49 One who's brand-conscious
50 Pleiades pursuer
51 Hawk
52 Fictional Flanders
55 Ditzy
57 Uttered
58 What Hamlet never called his mom
59 DeVille or Bonneville
60 They may get rattled

January

MARTIN LUTHER KING JR. DAY

monday

19   19

tuesday

20   20

wednesday

21   21

thursday

22   22

friday

23   23

saturday

24   24

s	m	t	w	t	f	s
				1	2	3
4	5	6	7	8	9	10
11	12	13	14	15	16	17
18	19	20	21	22	23	24
25	26	27	28	29	30	31

sunday

25   25

5. THE FRENCH CONNECTION

The New York Times

BY JOE DIPIETRO / EDITED BY WILL SHORTZ / 07-03-05

ACROSS

1 Georgia state wildflower
7 Georgia neighbor
14 1970's-80's singer Ronnie
20 Fixes, as a bow
21 Product usually used at night
22 New York lake
23 Puts to the test
24 Girls at the playground?
26 Word before and after "by," "on," or "to"
27 Subsist
29 It may be relative
30 Wheat ___
31 Rear parts of an article of radio equipment?
36 Big atlas section
38 Party person
39 Kind of race
40 "No way"
44 Hero
45 Rest on
47 Assails
50 Journalist Kupcinet
51 More than just a jaunt
53 Barely beats
54 Slow dance with quick turns
55 Provision of the Natl. Security Act, 1947
56 Grand ___ (wine appellation)
58 Golf club resembling an inverted V?
60 ___-Tiki
61 Retainers
63 Ones with potato peelers, for short
64 Break time
65 Shipping dept. stamp
66 First-aid item
68 "___ takers?"
69 Fume
71 Distillery items
72 Milk-related
76 2001 album with the #1 hit "Ain't It Funny"
79 Mass offering
80 Time ___
81 Metallic restraint on Baryshnikov?
83 Architectural feature
84 55-Across relative
85 Northeast tollroad option
86 Emasculate
88 Catty comeback
91 Symbol of slipperiness
92 Vikings' foes
93 Wore briefly
95 Map abbr.
96 Take out
98 Alliance
99 Con men often use them
101 The Baltics, once: Abbr.
103 Ball bearing on a spaceship?
105 Spot for a spare tire
108 Sister of Rachel
110 Cartoon dog
111 "Skip me"
112 Beneath a pendant opener?
117 Pretenses
120 Witnessed in the area of
121 What's left
122 Prom date
123 TV ratings period
124 Experimented with drugs, say
125 "National Velvet" star

DOWN

1 Ernst colleague
2 Time to attack
3 Present for your communication with an English saint?
4 Occupy
5 Like a really big shoe
6 Hired gun
7 Long suit
8 Range setting
9 "But who ___ to …?"
10 Coal holder
11 2002 World Series champs
12 Hills without peaks
13 Good fellers
14 Den ___
15 First-move maker
16 "When Your Child Drives You Crazy" author
17 "Sure thing" for Speedy Gonzales
18 Mideast's Gulf of ___
19 Part of a wagon train's route
25 Garden party, maybe
28 Order more of
32 ___ Arc, Ark.
33 Homers, slangily
34 Sprang up
35 Squirt
37 Ghosts or goblins
38 Presidential monogram
41 When some insects are cited for biting?
42 Sweet roll
43 Boxer Holyfield
46 Quickly, briefly
47 ___ de combat
48 Dismounted
49 Golfer Ballesteros

LUNAR NEW YEAR

monday 26 · 26

tuesday 27 · 27

wednesday 28 · 28

thursday 29 · 29

friday 30 · 30

saturday 31 · 31

sunday 1 · 32

s	m	t	w	t	f	s
1	2	3	4	5	6	7
8	9	10	11	12	13	14
15	16	17	18	19	20	21
22	23	24	25	26	27	28

FEBRUARY

The New York Times

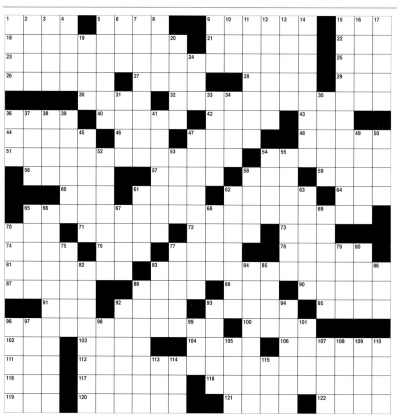

96 1960's presidential candi-
  date living overseas?
100 Small fry
102 Born, in Bretagne
103 Posterior
104 Title mom in a comic strip
106 Head home
111 Cape ___
112 Pain caused by adding
  onto a house?
116 Snappy 60's dresser
117 Pungent sandwich slice
118 Angling gear?
119 Powerbrokers
120 Burn up
121 ___ milk
122 Carved

DOWN

1 Makes accessible, old-
  style
2 Sumptuous
3 Chip on the table, maybe
4 Some RCA products
5 19th-century author whose
  father founded a utopian
  community
6 Band's place on
  Broadway
7 Sledder's protection
8 Architect Saarinen
9 "Now ___ theater near
  you!"
10 Swiss canton
11 Knights in competition
12 Winter chipper
13 Breakfast table staple:
  Var.
14 Tusked animal
15 "Get help!"
16 Loose
17 With 40-Across, a popular
  rental
19 Boaters and such
20 Baffled
24 "Top Hat" film studio
31 "Phooey!"
33 West Yorkshire city
34 Kitchen addition
35 Kind of sentence
36 Copy
37 Barber shop call
38 Rustic locale
39 Shrimp ___
41 Intense teaching programs
45 Anticipate
47 Taste-related
49 Prorate
50 Late July babies
52 Oscar night greeting

BY ELIZABETH C. GORSKI / EDITED BY WILL SHORTZ / 07-10-05

ACROSS

1 Scandinavian royal
5 Basilica area
9 Psychologist's study
15 Growler
18 If successful, they're
  laughed at
21 1970's White House
  name
22 Which card to pick,
  according to a magician
23 Films shown at dentists'
  conventions?
25 Bygone Ford
26 Handles
27 Captain Queeg's creator
28 Unloose
29 Make stuff up
30 Criteria: Abbr.
32 Shipper of Natalie's
  records abroad?
36 Common bonds

40 See 17-Down
42 To be, to Henri
43 "How obvious!"
44 Shalom
46 Feel fluish
47 Comprehends
48 N.B.A. star who starred
  in "Kazaam"
51 Disposition of a regular
  sort of person?
54 Accessory for the
  Penguin, in "Batman"
56 Allegro and vivace, e.g.
57 Bitter end?
58 Tyler of "Armageddon"
59 Court plea, for short
60 ___ curiam (by the court)
61 Waterfall feature
62 Buenos ___
64 Like an anode: Abbr.
65 Painter who makes a fast
  substitution?

70 "The Santa Clause,"
  for one
71 South Pacific carvings
72 Bullwinkle, e.g.
73 Muscle movement
74 Number two
76 A few: Abbr.
77 "Fargo" director
78 Home cooker
81 Forward thinker?
83 Commuter train
  eschewed by Dracula?
87 Bacon bit
88 Hollywood's Grant
89 "___-La-La"
  (1974 Al Green hit)
90 Seasons to be merry
91 Go downhill fast
92 Wilbur Post's horse
93 Union member
95 Dish eaten with a spork

February

monday
☽ 2 33

tuesday
3 34

wednesday
4 35

thursday
5 36

friday
6 37

saturday
7 38

sunday
8 39

s	m	t	w	t	f	s
1	2	3	4	5	6	7
8	9	10	11	12	13	14
15	16	17	18	19	20	21
22	23	24	25	26	27	28

7. NEW AR·RANGEMENTS

The New York Times

BY CON PEDERSON / EDITED BY WILL SHORTZ / 07-17-05

ACROSS

1 Regis Philbin or Kelly Ripa
7 Related on the father's side
13 Benefactor
19 "Forward!" in Italy
20 Number 1, e.g.
21 Distillate
22 Unmask
23 Supper at home before unpacking from a move?
25 "You're ___ friend"
26 Guinness superlative
27 Pipe contents
28 Founding Father listed on a popular computer?
33 Vinland pioneers
37 Suffix with Caesar
38 Cartoon dog
39 Rove
40 Constitutional
41 Old ___ (Satan)
43 Mild swearing competition?
49 Steps on the scale
50 Farrier's tool
52 Bargain repository
53 Connect with
54 American magazine founded in France
55 Old Colgate rival
57 All-Star team, with "the"
59 Part of E.E.C.: Abbr.
60 Divine one, to Dante
61 Shelters
64 Willa Cather's "One of ___"
66 Cuckoo bird
67 "This one's ___"
69 Prize for Coronado
70 Hurry up, as one decorating Christmas gifts?
74 Actress Scala
75 Red Cross inventories
77 Bill passer: Abbr.
78 Work on, in a way
79 Fire sources
81 Frequent abbr. in BBC announcements
82 Not give ___
84 1987 Pulitzer-winning critic Richard ___
86 Compact contents
87 Jack-in-the-pulpit, e.g.
88 Automaton of Hebrew lore
90 Art collector/ philanthropist ___ Broad
91 Working without ___
92 Latin American agreements
93 Like a test with a properly corrected score?
96 Guideline: Abbr.
98 Inner selves

DOWN

1 Wine order
2 Flooded
3 What the Beatles were able to do?
4 Early hr.
5 Like yesterday's news, to today's
6 Three Dog Night hit "___ the World Ends"
7 Wing
8 Mill stuff
9 Beethoven's symphony with "Ode to Joy"
10 Bird: Prefix
11 First in double figures
12 Joule fraction
13 Jr.'s test
14 Balloonists' trips
15 Eloise was a little one
16 Messenger with a code
17 Natl. Pretzel Mo.
18 Maiden-named
21 Carrier with blue-striped jets
24 Punch alternative
26 "Flash Gordon" villain ___ the Merciless
29 Take in
30 I problem?
31 Bonkers
32 "Frasier" terrier
34 Positioning the Trojan horse in front of Troy?
35 Zigzag activity
36 On the other hand
40 Less emotional
42 Philosopher Kierkegaard, e.g.

100 Recommendation from a C.P.A.
101 Fed. overseer
103 Magazine exec in PJ's
105 River to the Rio Grande
106 Improper trade of a St. Louis N.F.L. player?
112 Safari-goers may get a charge out of it
114 Think box
115 Quebec underground
116 Guests who jabber incessantly?
122 Less sweet
123 Haloes
124 Immediately
125 Box up
126 Undercover jobs
127 Use a straw
128 Experts

February

s	m	t	w	t	f	s
1	2	3	4	5	6	7
8	9	10	11	12	13	14
15	16	17	18	19	20	21
22	23	24	25	26	27	28

monday
9 40

tuesday
10 41

wednesday
11 42

thursday
12 43

friday
13 44

VALENTINE'S DAY
saturday
14 45

sunday
15 46

The New York Times

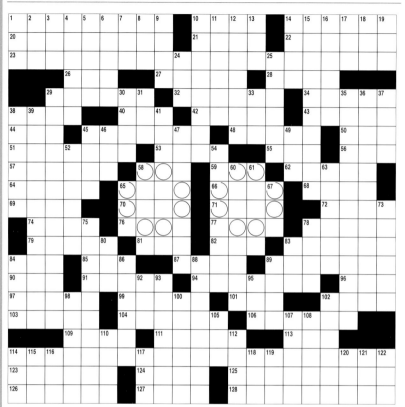

99 Famous fountain
101 Old Mideast grp.
102 ___ hall
103 Bacon piece
104 Offering relief
106 Eponymous doctor who
   studied hypnosis
109 Diner side
111 Movie chameleon of 1983
113 "Cultured insolence,"
   according to Aristotle
114 Any story in a certain
   movie serial ... or a
   75-Down attraction
123 Scout's interest
124 Auberges
125 Original price of
   admission to 75-Down
126 Overeater's plateful,
   sometimes
127 "I'll ___ brief as possible"
128 Age category of most college entrants

DOWN

1 Break
2 Valve opening?
3 Word with candy or drops
4 Works, as wet clay
5 ___ Range, in the West
6 Specialty
7 Miami duo?
8 "Baudolino" author
9 Call with outstretched
   arms
10 High ___
11 Ring of color
12 Sydney Carton's creator
13 Traveler's request: Abbr.
14 Averse to, in dialect
15 Matterhorn rider at
   75-Down
16 Dogfaced primate
17 Flamenco dancer's shout
18 Actress Carrere
19 Wallet item
24 Not yet scheduled, in
   schedules
25 Meet
29 Amusement park that was
   a model for 75-Down
30 It doesn't rain but it pours
31 ___ room
33 DVD player maker
35 TV personality who
   co-hosted the opening
   of 75-Down
36 Group that made their
   first TV appearance at
   the opening of 75-Down

BY DAVID J. KAHN / EDITED BY WILL SHORTZ / 07-24-05

ACROSS

1 Club charges for non-
   members
10 One-named singer
14 Straight man of comedy
20 P.O. address of 75-Down
21 Lit ___ (college course)
22 Athlete in a crease
23 2003 action movie ... or
   a 75-Down attraction
26 Party person
27 Where to find a
   story online
28 Not ___ many words
29 Sensitive
32 Some people who send
   I.M.'s
34 Rich soils
38 Reformer born in Denmark
40 Trap
42 Armstrong on wheels
43 Join, with "in"

44 Part of S.A.S.E.: Abbr.
45 Pull off
48 Filled up
50 Yours, in Italy
51 Properly lined up
53 Certain dweller on the
   Danube
55 Statute: Abbr.
56 Beach sight in W.W. II:
   Abbr.
57 Ratio marks
58 Presumptions
59 Bring up, as a grievance
62 "Aladdin" role
64 Musical with the song
   "Rainbow Tour"
65 Kind of party
66 One of the baseball
   Boones
68 Have value
69 Dreamcast game maker
70 Mata ___ (spy)

71 "You betcha"
72 Bias
74 Aromatic herb used by
   the ancients
76 To ___ (perfectly)
77 Movie shot
78 Mediterranean cruise stop
79 Mealtime plea to junior
81 Part of Lombard Street
   in San Francisco
82 Gray matter?
83 Astronaut Collins
84 Nod, maybe
85 ___ Locks
87 2004 sword-and-sandals
   flick
89 Took by force
90 Eggs in water?
91 Observant one
94 Torch carriers?
96 Sung syllable
97 Avril is part of it

February

s	m	t	w	t	f	s
1	2	3	4	5	6	7
8	9	10	11	12	13	14
15	16	17	18	19	20	21
22	23	24	25	26	27	28

PRESIDENTS' DAY

monday
(16   47

tuesday
17   48

wednesday
18   49

thursday
19   50

friday
20   51

saturday
21   52

sunday
22   53

9. A LOT OF CHOICES

BY FRANK LONGO / EDITED BY WILL SHORTZ / 07-31-05

ACROSS

1 Euripides heroine
8 Soyuz cosmonaut Makarov
12 Tending to radiate
20 Snow-white dog
21 Part of N.B.
22 Got going
23 Risky marketing of sports jackets on a city's outskirts? [Chevrolet]
26 It comes out in the wash
27 "This guy walks into ___ ..."
28 Apollo mission vehicle
29 Cowpoke, often
30 More than a sip
32 "Bad Behavior" star, 1993
34 Result of teasing?
38 Understanding of how to keep peace in the community? [Honda]
45 Fell
48 Dance springily
49 "Rock and Roll, Hoochie ___"
50 His "Parade" included parts for typewriter, foghorn and rattle
51 Suffix with planet
52 Western native
53 Storting meeting place
55 Locale of some hangings: Abbr.
57 Zippo
58 Some underwear
59 Aura surrounding a black mountain lion? [Mercury]
64 One option for Hamlet
65 Garage supply
66 Deck material
67 N.H.L.'s ___ Trophy
70 Some claimants
73 Shooter Adams
75 Token
76 "Bewitched" witch
77 Harsh call
78 "Third Watch" actress Texada
80 Exiled African leader
81 Search for poetry in the Old West? [Nissan]
86 Its point is guarded
88 Sitter's acquisition
89 Volume 1 heading starter
90 Astronomer's study
91 Eavesdropping org.
92 Story
93 Hotel employee
95 Subj. for U.S. newcomers
97 Half seas over
98 Deck (out)
99 Fearless group of traveling sheep? [Dodge]
104 Moralistic declaration
105 Simile part
106 Prefix with cop, in a film title
109 Grandma at a bar mitzvah
112 Noted apple pie baker
114 Stretch
117 Daughter of Saturn
119 Accompany a horse researcher? [Ford]
125 Lobster may be served in it
126 Blue hue
127 Glimpses
128 Lake Michigan arm
129 Georgetown athlete
130 Baptisms of fire

DOWN

1 Petrol brand
2 Heaps kudos on
3 Form into an arch, old-style
4 TV personality with a voice in "Shark Tale"
5 Norse war god
6 Musical McEntire
7 Not much at all
8 Temporarily punched out
9 Cyber-chortle
10 Card catalog abbr.
11 Shady resting place
12 Labyrinth locale
13 Early 12th-century year
14 Resident: Suffix
15 Daily event
16 Zen goal
17 "Give ___ for ..."
18 "Billy Budd" captain
19 Pulitzer-winning critic Richard
24 Figure in a bust
25 Mideast parley attenders
31 Fatigued action figure?
33 In ___ (really out of it)
35 Polish part
36 Number-starting cry
37 Kind of dye
39 Baron's superior: Abbr.
40 Homes with domes
41 Judiciary
42 "The whole of ___ consists in the art of being honest": Jefferson
43 Lay low
44 Lions' goals, briefly
45 Get the lead out
46 ___ shrdlu
47 Goose steppers?
54 Not non
56 Barrie buccaneer
58 42-Down division

Feb/Mar

monday
23 54

MARDI GRAS
tuesday
24 55

ASH WEDNESDAY
wednesday
25 56

thursday
26 57

friday
27 58

saturday
28 59

sunday
1 60

s	m	t	w	t	f	s
1	2	3	4	5	6	7
8	9	10	11	12	13	14
15	16	17	18	19	20	21
22	23	24	25	26	27	28
29	30	31				

MARCH

10. PUZZLED EXPRESSION

The New York Times

BY MARK FELDMAN / EDITED BY WILL SHORTZ / 08-06-05

ACROSS

1 Ballpark figures
5 Tourer with Carreras and Domingo
14 Genesis event, with "the"
18 Notarized doc., e.g.
19 Egg drop?
20 Lower small intestines
21 Kowtow
23 Doesn't cry uncle
24 Basketry material
25 One who's far from a fan
27 Like shrinking violets
28 Cordovan and kid, e.g.
30 Camaraderies
32 French mathematician Marin ___
33 Image depicted by this puzzle, after it's solved
34 Throng
38 Some cosmetics
40 Conseco Fieldhouse team
41 Bidding doers
43 One with a nice bod
44 It has moles: Abbr.
45 While getting there
46 Calendar mo.
47 Not practiced
50 Bit of workout gear
52 Symbols of happiness
54 "Huh-uh"
56 Something noticed at a fish market
57 Essential nutrient
59 Primrose variety
62 Sniff around
63 Refuse receptacle
67 Day's end: Abbr.
68 Spreadsheet fill
70 Fair feature
71 Vane dir.
72 Agnus ___
73 Come out of denial
76 Gershwin musical
78 Env. contents
79 Joule parts
81 Slight irregularities
83 Ran while wet
84 Clown's cover-up
88 Really roughs up
89 Dignity restorer
92 Thin mug with sharp features
94 Bill of Rights subj.
95 Compact things
97 Giant of a Giant
98 Hand holder?
100 It's not necessarily the real worth
102 Go for the gold?
103 Helmsman's headache
105 Was in a meet, maybe
106 Take ___ (drop off briefly)
107 Bean source
108 Hair feature
110 Memorable times
112 Senior airman's superior: Abbr.
113 Hindu wonder-worker: Var.
114 Heroine in Bizet's "The Pearl Fishers"
115 Ones in charge: Abbr.
116 Conference start?
117 Regular
118 Novelist O'Brien and others
119 Out-of-commission cruisers: Abbr.
120 Operates
121 Feels dizzy

DOWN

1 School in La Jolla: Abbr.
2 She might cite you
3 Commonplace
4 Cork up
5 Look that says nothing
6 Forestall
7 Somme sight
8 European river source
9 Ill-considered
10 "Our Gang" affirmative
11 Wee warbler
12 Transparent linen
13 Communicate (with)
14 Stocking stuff
15 Unpleasant sort
16 Jack Lemmon's "Days of Wine and Roses" co-star
17 Metallica drummer Ulrich
22 Proverbial payee
24 County whose seat is Alamogordo
26 Tamari sauce and the like
29 "The Nazarene" novelist
31 Stands out significantly
32 Like some blocks
33 Provider of creature comforts?: Abbr.
35 Cloverleaf component
36 Water cannon target
37 Twice
39 Goes down
41 Litter box cry
42 "D-OH" person, e.g.
48 Those with clout
49 Title type, often
50 Anatomical dividers
51 Finished off
52 Be humiliated
53 Antenna holder
55 Singer called "The Little Sparrow"
58 First name of "America's Mayor"

March

59 Give up
60 Afflicted with root rot, perhaps
61 Repeatedly raise the bar?
64 Period of high artistic development
65 Ethnically diverse
66 Mathlete, stereotypically
69 Oberhausen outburst
70 "Angels of mercy," briefly
74 Broadway lyricist Rice
75 Gangster moniker
76 Not in profile
77 Airborne Express alternative
80 Quotation qualification
82 Nod, maybe
83 Letters on undies
85 Marijuana's chief intoxicant: Abbr.
86 Aquatic zappers
87 Smallish items on rods
89 Surrounders of light switches
90 Extra horsepower, slangily
91 Electrify
92 Limp
93 King and queen
95 Formation between two edges of a polyhedron
96 Pound sounds
99 Target alternative
101 Glad supporters
104 ___ monster
107 Matter for a judge
109 107-Down assignees, for short
111 Lottery-running org.
112 Three-time World Series of Poker champ ___ Ungar
113 Warm covering

monday

2 61

tuesday

3 62

wednesday

☽ 4 63

thursday

5 64

friday

6 65

saturday

7 66

s	m	t	w	t	f	s
1	2	3	4	5	6	7
8	9	10	11	12	13	14
15	16	17	18	19	20	21
22	23	24	25	26	27	28
29	30	31				

INTERNATIONAL WOMEN'S DAY
DAYLIGHT SAVING TIME BEGINS

sunday

8 67

The New York Times

By Lee Glickstein and Nany Salomom / Edited by Will Shortz / 08-14-05

ACROSS

1 Court case?
8 Friendly correspondent
14 Toy that goes "bang"
20 Rocket stage
21 Develop
22 Melodic
23 Protection in the city?
25 Cut with the grain
26 Playwright O'Casey
27 Keep out
28 Surfer stops
30 Work unit
31 Traditional brain doctor?
37 Thingums
39 Singer Jarreau and others
40 Take in
41 Pique
42 Nantes-to-Paris dir.
43 Brood
45 Convention V.I.P.'s
48 What Indian cooks play?
53 Tide competitor
54 Mystique
55 California river named for a fish
56 Major injustice
59 Historic plane
62 Home of a '69 "miracle"
64 Decent fellow
68 PC display
69 Federal government connections?
73 Sob syllable
74 Australian lass
76 Mavens
77 Try to snow
79 Sheet fabric
82 Iranian ayatollah Sayyed ___ Khamenei
83 Panhandle migrant
84 Work for eds.
86 Schedule at a Vegas chapel?
91 George Washington University athletes
94 Backside
95 Indivisible
96 "Double Fantasy" singer
97 Producer of lts.
98 Tokyo carrier, for short
99 Adam and Eve, presumably
103 Sodom or Gomorrah?
109 Cry of wonder
110 Goes first
111 Thimbleful
112 Swing around
113 Scanty, in Scarborough
115 Result of wearing high heels?
120 Get to
121 Be upset by, say
122 Purified, as water
123 Cordwood units
124 Like slander
125 "Timon of Athens," e.g.

DOWN

1 Was addicted to
2 Lord of the ring?
3 English-speaking island in the Caribbean
4 ___ aside
5 Smoker's purchase: Abbr.
6 "___ let us in, knows where we've been" (Beatles lyric)
7 Cavern on the way to Hades
8 California's San ___ Bay
9 Modern music genre
10 ___ Tamid (synagogue lamp)
11 Some scampi
12 Infamous 1972 hurricane
13 Don't bother
14 Desert parade
15 Thank you, in Tokyo
16 Lab tube
17 Dirt spreader
18 Can. neighbor
19 "I said ___!"
24 It might go for a dip in the ocean
29 Wolf or shark
31 When repeated, Mork's TV sign-off
32 Linda of "Jekyll & Hyde"
33 ___ Andy ("Show Boat" role)
34 First name in fashion
35 Miles of film
36 Some warriors in "War of the Worlds"
38 Transfer
43 "As if!"
44 Salad topper
45 Where "South Pacific" was filmed
46 CPR giver
47 Bar mitzvah boy, for one
48 Asian weight units
49 Suspicion
50 Lose ground?
51 Behind
52 Busy people
57 Singing brothers' name
58 Daring deed
60 Fit
61 ___ gum (thickening agent)
62 More likely
63 Where to dig "Six Feet Under"
65 Plumed hat

March

PURIM (BEGINS AT SUNSET)

monday
9 68

tuesday
10 69

wednesday
○ **11** 70

thursday
12 71

friday
13 72

saturday
14 73

sunday
15 74

s	m	t	w	t	f	s
1	2	3	4	5	6	7
8	9	10	11	12	13	14
15	16	17	18	19	20	21
22	23	24	25	26	27	28
29	30	31				

BY PATRICK MERRELL / EDITED BY WILL SHORTZ / 08-21-05

ACROSS

1 Mathematical fig.
5 Whistler, e.g.
11 Cargo platform
15 Chatter
18 ___ pneumonia
19 Stephen Foster's dream girl
20 Pro's opposite
21 Arapaho foe
22 Life saver
25 French law
26 Puzzles
27 "Survivor" sight
28 Sonar pulse
29 "Is that so?!"
30 King of England in 1700
36 "Lord, is ___?"
38 Without interruption
39 Perfume amounts
40 Critical tennis situation
45 Bygone nuclear agcy.
46 Monstrous
48 Stingers
51 Money substitute, for short
54 Timeline divisions
55 Prop for the Acad. Awards
56 Supreme finale
57 Launch sites
59 "Stay!"
62 Waterfall jumper
66 Rustic couple
68 Sidekick of old children's TV
71 Idle talk
74 Jawaharlal Nehru's daughter
75 Nearby
79 Flour cake
80 Like NyQuil: Abbr.
82 Actress Gardner
84 Stick in a dish
85 Tahoe, for one
86 Plant expert?
93 Proofers' catches
95 Nashville-based awards org.
96 Watch
97 Hurting
99 Horseshoe-shaped wear
101 Delta wing craft
102 Duke Ellington classic
106 Ballerina Karsavina
111 Big hands often take them
112 Musician Brian
113 Waters
115 First name in despotism
116 Tanning agents
121 ___-mo
122 33-Down's home today
123 Sister of Erato
124 Lace tip
125 Natural incubator
126 Masked one, informally
127 Bible parts
128 Diner in "Alice"

DOWN

1 His last words were "Thus with a kiss I die"
2 Critic with a Hollywood Walk of Fame star
3 ___ diem (motto of Horace)
4 13-figure figure
5 Sophocles drama
6 Extend
7 Putts out
8 Pasta suffix
9 Failing
10 Shatner's "___ War"
11 Run one's fingers over
12 1997 treaty city
13 ___ agent
14 Bashes
15 1960's-70's PBS star
16 Now
17 Considers
18 "Lethal Weapon" force: Abbr.
23 Like the fire goddess Brigit
24 Famed political hanger-on
28 Female swans
31 Soil layer
32 Actor ___ Cobb
33 Ancient people
34 Stronghold
35 Powerful
37 Court case title phrase
40 It's involved in many spills
41 Architect Saarinen
42 Certain fraud investigator, informally
43 Daily neighborhood sight
44 Ex-lax?
46 Some nods
47 "You'll never ___!"
49 Cupidity
50 Not extreme
52 "Alley ___"
53 Letters on a stamp
58 Briefly
60 Care, slangily
61 Suffix with verb
63 KO insert?
64 50-Down: Prefix
65 Clandestine maritime org.
67 Baseball club designation
69 Brookie or laker
70 Diner cupfuls
71 Mail addenda, for short

monday
16 75

ST. PATRICK'S DAY   *tuesday*
17 76

wednesday
☾ **18** 77

thursday
19 78

VERNAL EQUINOX 11:44 UTC   *friday*
20 79

saturday
21 80

MOTHERING SUNDAY (UK)   *sunday*
22 81

s	m	t	w	t	f	s
1	2	3	4	5	6	7
8	9	10	11	12	13	14
15	16	17	18	19	20	21
22	23	24	25	26	27	28
29	30	31				

13. THE MAMAS AND THE PAPAS

BY BYRON WALDEN / EDITED BY WILL SHORTZ / 08-28-05

ACROSS

1 It's the top
5 Medieval chest
9 Energy ___
13 Ideally
19 Puts in one's place
21 Rwandan people
22 Place to store food
23 Hardly snug attire
25 Take offense
26 1967 war participant: Abbr.
27 Harley, slangily
28 Walruses and whales
30 Marker
32 Alternatives to lattes
34 Messenger ___
35 Hawaiian bigeye
37 Dove, for one
46 Some are hidden
49 "If ___ you ..."
50 Light into
51 The City of Churches
52 Basketball commentator Dick
54 Face trouble
55 Lustrous fabrics
56 What major retailers do
59 Discomfit
60 Ram
61 Suffix with cine
62 Effeminate
63 Dramatic medium
66 Car that won the 1939 and 1940 Indianapolis 500
69 Journal ending
71 National symbol of Wales
72 Whittle
73 Brown shade
76 Works on a car's alignment?
80 Arc producer
82 Impertinent one
83 Friend of Peppermint Patty
84 Slip out of class
85 Striped African animals
88 Like the mumps
89 Trials
90 Store overseers
93 Title of respect
94 Actress Meyers
95 "Mighty stream so deep and wide," in song
98 To be, to Brutus
101 Sleepovers
109 Morgue, for one
111 Bill producer, for short
112 Literary critic Trilling
113 Tabloid nickname for Sydney Biddle Barrows
116 Largest city on the island Fyn
117 AOL and others
118 Remote power source?
119 "The Kingdom and the Power" author
120 "Out!"
121 Article II subj.
122 Requires

DOWN

1 Glaze for fish dishes
2 Go at it
3 Mr. Right, say
4 Grp. setting standards
5 Not standing
6 Approximate
7 100 lbs.
8 Shortage of punch
9 Blacken
10 Tribe noted for its silver and turquoise jewelry
11 Env. directive
12 Stratagem
13 Neighbor of Macedonia
14 Places for taking off
15 Cup part
16 Source for Wagner's "The Ring of the Nibelung"
17 Leave the shelves
18 "___ intéressant"
20 P.T.A. concern
24 Coat, as metal, to reduce its chemical reactivity
29 Actor who played Santa with Nancy Reagan in his lap
31 Flogging
33 Abbey area
36 Emotionally withdrawn
38 See 101-Down
39 Subject heading in a hotel brochure
40 Composer Khachaturian
41 Disappointing return
42 "The hour ___ hand"
43 Community abutting Santa Monica
44 Swedish taxonomist Carl von ___
45 Gray lines?
46 Very little
47 Cartoonist Browne
48 Pitches
51 Computer pioneer Lovelace
53 Film director ___ C. Kenton
56 Schnoz site
57 Plop preceder
58 Case studies, e.g.
60 Treat with honey
64 Poivre's partner
65 Crawl (with)

March

monday
23
82

tuesday
24
83

wednesday
25
84

thursday
26
85

friday
27
86

saturday
28
87

s	m	t	w	t	f	s
1	2	3	4	5	6	7
8	9	10	11	12	13	14
15	16	17	18	19	20	21
22	23	24	25	26	27	28
29	30	31				

SUMMER TIME BEGINS (UK)

sunday
29
88

MARCH

The New York Times

BY NANCY NICHOLSON JOLINE / EDITED BY WILL SHORTZ / 09-04-05

ACROSS

1 Turkic people
7 Series of movements
13 Patient form info
16 Baron von Trapp
21 It may be folded for breakfast
22 Part of Isabella I's realm
23 Sch. in Kingston
24 Connecticut or Delaware
25 How this answer is situated
27 Nothing
28 "Gladiator" setting
29 Cookout aid
30 Eyelid afflictions
32 Eventually
34 Thatching material
36 Irene ___ ("A Scandal in Bohemia" woman)
38 Seventh-century Arab caliph
39 March cry
40 Paul Anka #1 hit
43 Must
46 Flighty sort?
48 Fuel suffix
49 Up
50 How this answer is situated
52 Purplish
53 Water carrier
54 Cassini and others
55 Some mil. careerists
56 Decorative fabrics
58 Basilica feature
59 Shave
60 How this answer is situated
63 Beer bash need
64 Like Nehru jackets
66 Made known
70 Possible backache cause
74 "Dies ___"
75 Shepherd's pie ingredients
77 It gets a licking
78 Goof-offs
79 Out of memory?
81 Rennes resident
83 Gaze dreamily
84 Sight from Taormina
86 Messieurs' mates: Abbr.
87 Belly-dancers' accouterments
88 "Heat" co-star, 1995
91 Gounod opera
92 "If the ___ is concealed, it succeeds": Ovid
93 How this answer is situated
96 Long
98 Certain sorority member
102 Summer Olympics racers
105 Wannabe, often
106 Got up
107 "What a pity!"
108 Normandy river
109 How this answer is situated
112 Time
113 Topper
114 Faculties
116 Finish second
117 Resembling a beanpole
118 Suffix with Capri
119 Identify
120 Prefix with comic
122 Reference book for a writer

125 Charles who founded an investment firm
127 Start of many sequel titles
129 Derelict
132 "That's an ___!"
133 Oneself
136 How this answer is situated
140 Weeper of myth
141 Pal of Rover
142 Prayer
143 Two-timing
144 Thick novels
145 Censor's target
146 African scourge
147 Ostensible

DOWN

1 Boatload
2 Actor Leon of "Life With Father"
3 Sermon's basis
4 Sub
5 Camp David, e.g.
6 Curling item
7 ___ Paulo
8 Leftover morsel
9 Casual turndowns
10 Hurried, musically
11 "Leave It to Beaver" actor
12 Sweetheart
13 Barbarian
14 Diagnostic aid, for short
15 Wick holder
16 Au ___
17 Limerick locale
18 How this answer is situated
19 Give up
20 Scholarship winners
26 Doze
31 Rap session?
33 ___ maison (indoors): Fr.
35 Farrier
37 Severity
40 1910's-20's movement
41 Live ___
42 Fundamentals
44 Zouave, by birth
45 Some Mercedes-Benzes
47 Seller of Alaska, 1867
50 Ernest who designed Washington's Corcoran gallery
51 Fascinated by
52 Goes through
54 Starts the betting
56 Cask control
57 Reproductive cells
60 ___ impasse
61 Ex-con
62 ___ Bounty
63 Red apéritif
65 Columnist Bombeck
67 Haul
68 Organic compound

Mar/Apr

monday
30
89

tuesday
31
90

wednesday
1
91

thursday
☽ # 2
92

friday
3
93

saturday
4
94

PALM SUNDAY

sunday
5
95

s	m	t	w	t	f	s
			1	2	3	4
5	6	7	8	9	10	11
12	13	14	15	16	17	18
19	20	21	22	23	24	25
26	27	28	29	30		

APRIL

15. SPEAKING CANADIAN

BY RICHARD SILVESTRI / EDITED BY WILL SHORTZ / 09-11-05

ACROSS

1 Toot one's horn
5 Make run smoothly again
10 Cellar container
14 Calculating folks?
18 See 65-Across
19 Turned up
20 Helm position
21 Used cars
22 French artist's vacation spot?
24 Masculine principle
25 Holly plant
26 Long in movies
27 Ecclesiastical setback?
28 Track of a sort
30 Formal response to "Who's there?"
31 Really blue
34 Browning work?
35 Bigoted bunch
37 Go-ahead
38 Prestige of Jay's predecessor?
40 Medical tube
41 Elaborate entertainment
44 Social register word
45 Actress Thurman
46 Tums alternative
49 Kneecap
53 Rural horse-drawn conveyance
57 Fancy fabric for Darius the Great?
60 "The Simpsons" creator Groening
62 They sit on the dais
64 1972 top 10 hit going over seven minutes
65 With 18-Across, Tijuana goodbye
66 Went at it
67 Dress style
69 "Hey …!"
70 Started a hole
71 Bird for the table
73 Stockpiling
75 Time long past
76 Dr. Jekyll's flooring?
79 Opposite of exo-
80 Ann or Andy
82 Mosey
84 "… boy ___ girl?"
85 Palm Sunday mount
88 Score unit
89 Forgets about
94 Fish surgeon?
99 1964 Hitchcock film
100 Apple pie order?
101 Be in misery
102 Part of a flight
105 Young Turk
106 Not presto
108 Like beds, at times
109 Leaving after lunch
110 Long-toed bird with a harsh cry
111 Attired
112 Pasta that will make you really sick?
116 White-tailed eagle
117 Coil in the yard
118 Record
119 Admiral's command
120 The Big Board, for short
121 Still-life subject
122 Seeder name
123 Buffalo Bill

DOWN

1 Adjective for Atlanta's Hartsfield airport
2 Backslide
3 Time of one's life
4 Sticky stuff
5 Deadens acoustically
6 Not leave one's mark
7 Brushed (up)
8 Bring to bear
9 Irritates
10 Hot pepper
11 Presidential middle name
12 One whose speech is halting
13 One tapped for a fraternity
14 Important pool shot?
15 Buff
16 Carol opening
17 Discriminatory, in a way
18 Blair and Hamilton
23 Firmly secured
29 "High Hopes" lyricist
30 "Veni," translated
32 Chihuahua on TV
33 ___'acte
36 Intense
38 Council member in "Star Wars"
39 Where the so-called "Roof of the World" is
41 Beat it
42 Toreador's reward
43 Frank McCourt memoir
47 Not a news piece
48 City near Monterey Bay
50 G.P. grp.
51 Part of LIFO, in accounting
52 Be there
53 Not quite legit
54 "Scream" genre
55 Soft wool
56 Welcome words to a fight promoter?
58 Tandoori-baked bread
59 Soapmaker's need
61 "Adios Muchachos," e.g.

April

monday

6 96

tuesday

7 97

PASSOVER (BEGINS AT SUNSET) *wednesday*

8 98

thursday

○ **9** 99

GOOD FRIDAY *friday*

10 100

saturday

11 101

s	m	t	w	t	f	s
			1	2	3	4
5	6	7	8	9	10	11
12	13	14	15	16	17	18
19	20	21	22	23	24	25
26	27	28	29	30		

APRIL

EASTER *sunday*

12 102

16. MAKING A LEFT

The New York Times

BY PATRICK BERRY / EDITED BY WILL SHORTZ / 09-18-05

ACROSS

1 Much-used engine
7 Spring from a bed
12 "Twin Peaks" victim ___ Palmer
17 Nose-puckering, in a way
18 See 37A
21 Lay concern?
22 Pulmotor's purpose
25 Diplomatic successes
26 Comerica Park team
27 Ab ___ (from the beginning)
30 Some Ouija answers
31 Unhuman
35 Dog in Francis Barraud's painting "His Master's Voice"
37 With 59A, 18D and 18A, what these answers show
41 "___ Enchanted" (Newbery-winning book made into a 2004 film)
42 Troubled
43 No longer reliant on mother
44 Where many barrels are seen
47 Greases
48 Pained reaction
49 Within walking distance
51 Fix a track
52 Practicing grp.
53 Somewhat, slangily
54 "Goodness Had Nothing to Do With It" autobiographer
56 Many a computer icon
59 See 37A
61 See 62D
65 "Stop that!"
66 Overly glib
67 Borrower
68 With 27D, what these answers show
69 See 92A
74 Crave
75 Drank some coffee, say, with "up"
77 Long arm
79 Yossarian's tentmate, in "Catch-22"
80 Mgr.'s holding
83 "Two Women" star
84 "À ___ santé!"
85 Educator Montessori
87 Sandwich's title?
89 Enter all at once
90 Ancient Mexican
91 ___ function
92 With 69A and 69D, what these answers show
95 Certifiable
96 Musical wingding
99 Marvin Gaye's "___ That Peculiar"
101 Old Ford
102 Window flankers
103 No longer with us
107 Disaster coverage?
114 "Almost Famous" director, 2000
115 Confirms
116 Knit up again
117 While away
118 "In dreams begin responsibility" writer
119 Hose

DOWN

1 Student's stat.
2 Lord's Prayer starter
3 Giant at Cooperstown
4 Photomap overlay
5 Firefighters hold them outside windows
6 Correctional worker?
7 Preside over
8 Galley's many
9 Sport ___
10 Artemis, to Apollo
11 Debate club fodder
12 Pick up
13 More nervous
14 German-speaking Swiss canton
15 Young 'un in the Hundred Acre Wood
16 "Roman Holiday" princess
18 See 37A
19 Plant chewed in Arabia
20 Sleepwear
23 Semicircular shape
24 Stephen of "FeardotCom"
27 See 68A
28 Another name for retinol
29 One whose working days are numbered
31 Air or field starter
32 Ignoramus
33 Baseball's Felipe
34 Souvlaki meat
36 Calculator part
38 Good to have around
39 Bivouacked
40 Percentage of a legal settlement
43 La Belle Époque ender: Abbr.
45 Serviceability
46 Unlikely Scottish sight
49 Berkeley university nickname

April

s	m	t	w	t	f	s
			1	2	3	4
5	6	7	8	9	10	11
12	13	14	15	16	17	18
19	20	21	22	23	24	25
26	27	28	29	30		

APRIL

EASTER MONDAY (CANADA, UK)

monday
13 103

tuesday
14 104

wednesday
15 105

thursday
16 106

friday
☾ 17 107

saturday
18 108

sunday
19 109

17. CRY ME A RIVER

The New York Times

BY JOE DIPIETRO / EDITED BY WILL SHORTZ / 09-25-05

ACROSS

1 ___ lab
4 Drunk
8 Whole lot
12 Pluck
18 One may be overhead or underfoot
19 Holding
21 Cut back
22 Greetings from the Far West?
23 Judge's cry?
26 Edit
27 Like some winter wear
28 Hides from view
29 Manicotti ingredient
30 Ignores
32 Coastal raptors
33 One making lots of money
34 Kind of grass
35 Envier's cry?
39 Informal evening
40 Came of age
43 "___ enough …"
44 Knowing
45 Titter
46 One might be a pull-out
50 F on a questionnaire, e.g.
51 Head of l'Académie
52 Unit of fat
53 Parishioner's cry?
58 Computer unit, informally
60 Door part
61 Antitank weapon
62 Miss, e.g.
64 Recluse's cry?
69 Beauty
70 Hole in the head
72 Deprive of courage
73 School basics, initially
75 New York sports fan's cry?
79 "My bad"
82 Place where there might be a mess
83 Card player's declaration
84 Coachmen : horses :: bullwhackers : ___
86 Brazen one
87 Richard of "Chicago"
88 A school might be found using it
90 Latter-day Aristotle
92 Nonstarters
93 Detroit sports fan's cry?
97 Outdoor sealant
98 Move, in real estate
99 Create, as a CD
100 Game sites
104 Single
106 Molded, as metal
109 Comedy Central's "The ___ Show"
110 Be a go-between
111 Racer's cry?

113 Printer type
114 One of the Waughs
115 Sexy Beatles lady
116 Certain Beatle's lady
117 Stop
118 Cotton fabric
119 ___ room
120 Dashiell Hammett character ___ Beaumont

DOWN

1 Whimsical
2 Peep show picture
3 Contract bridge?
4 Uncovered
5 Service arm: Abbr.
6 Onetime French fleet
7 Dastardly laugh
8 Other halves
9 Tout
10 Transgresses
11 Soaked
12 Corps member
13 Pick
14 Hurly-burly
15 Valley girl's cry?
16 Make milk
17 Home with a groundskeeper, maybe
20 ___ incognita
24 1991 Madonna hit
25 Quadrennial polit. event
29 Frost-covered
31 Suffix with butyl
33 Centennial of the Selma civil rights march
36 Fingers, to so speak
37 Window part
38 Ancient theaters
39 Explosion maker
40 Listing on a business sched.
41 ___ Lingus
42 Fatalist's cry?
44 Rock group with the 1995 hit "Buddy Holly"
47 Actress Lena
48 Roman, e.g.
49 Medea rode on it
51 Eliot Ness, for one
54 Society event
55 Black
56 Scratch (out)
57 Often-candied vegetable
59 Clear the throat?
60 Blessed
62 Venue for the Not Ready for Prime Time Players, in brief
63 Bladed tool

April

65 Fretted instrument
66 Laura's "La Gioconda" lover
67 Discover competitor
68 Do some modern surgery
71 Peter and others
74 "The Social Contract"
   philosopher
76 As much as you please
77 Roger Maris's number
78 Little biter
80 Last Greek consonant
81 Op opener
85 Eggy beverage
86 Highlight providers
87 Type of nucleotide
88 "You've got yourself a deal"
89 Kirstie's "Cheers" role
91 Colt fan's org.
92 Unexcitable
93 Old humorist ___ Burgess
94 Greatly
95 Coal cars
96 Clothing line
98 Blush alternatives
101 Coolpix camera maker
102 Deserted
103 Church council
105 Pacific island nation
106 "Burning Giraffe" painter
107 Couple
108 Motion in the ocean
111 Oil well feature
112 Underwater steerer

monday

20   110

tuesday

21   111

EARTH DAY   *wednesday*

22   112

thursday

23   113

friday

24   114

saturday

● 25   115

s	m	t	w	t	f	s
			1	2	3	4
5	6	7	8	9	10	11
12	13	14	15	16	17	18
19	20	21	22	23	24	25
26	27	28	29	30		

sunday

26   116

APRIL

The New York Times

BY MATT SKOCZEN / EDITED BY WILL SHORTZ / 10-02-05

ACROSS

1 Dog's owner
7 Crit. condition areas
11 Go (for)
14 Famed Chicago hotel
19 Station number
20 Injured, in a way
22 Like an apartment with new tenants
23 Dislodging boats that have run aground?
25 Runs for no purpose
26 Long stretch
27 Go for the gold?
28 Actress MacDowell
29 Beehives, e.g.
30 One calling at peak times?
33 Salon worker
35 "Horton Hears ___"
37 Advice to a husband seeker?
42 "Lowdown" singer Boz ___
45 Photo ID?
46 Chinese philosopher Chu ___
47 Respecting
48 Goddess of agriculture
49 Warm wool
52 Presidential monogram
54 "Don't ___ dumb"
55 Karaoke?
61 TKO caller
62 Get
64 Stairstep measure
65 Spots
67 Dart
69 Medical worker in a billfold picture?
74 Mex. miss
75 Glass component
77 It may follow a def.
78 WB competitor
80 One of the Ewings, on "Dallas"
81 Selective Service System, once?
86 Be bombastic
88 Hellenic vowel
89 Shows homage
90 First airline with commercial transpacific passenger flights
91 Lee foe
95 Football linemen: Abbr.
98 Melbourne-to-Brisbane dir.
99 [Not again!] and [I can't!]
100 Procrastinator's pick-up line?
105 Like venison
106 Annual Sunday night event, with "the"
107 Insignia

111 Bruce who appeared in "Suspicion"
113 Travis who sang "Here's a Quarter (Call Someone Who Cares)"
115 Comfy footwear
116 Shade of green
117 "We Help Heal" sloganeer
118 Where to store extra chandeliers?
122 Teacher's note on a test
123 Subject to change in size, as a picture on a screen
124 Famous Indy 500 family
125 Neil Armstrong's middle name
126 Halifax hrs.
127 Crosswalk users, for short
128 Shirley who sang "Goldfinger"

DOWN

1 Walk leisurely
2 Blessing preceder
3 Lose a lap
4 1960's chess champ Mikhail
5 Blow-up: Abbr.
6 Goes back into business
7 Library cataloging datum, briefly
8 PC "brain"
9 ___ Minor
10 Hélène, for one
11 Mark of a ruler
12 Money replaced by euros
13 QB stats
14 Icicle feature
15 1984 Patrick Swayze film, the first movie released with a PG-13 rating
16 "I'll do that"
17 Original Clarabell the Clown player
18 Brief strangers?
21 Its national anthem is "Jana Gana Mana"
24 Imperfection
29 Modern address
31 Beats (out)
32 Accesses the Web
34 Hebrew name meaning "He is my God"
36 Can. province
38 Kind of skirt
39 Kitchen item: Abbr.
40 Perfume holder
41 They make people raise their hands
42 Gobbles (up)
43 Historical novelist Holland

monday
27   ₁₁₇

tuesday
28   ₁₁₈

wednesday
29   ₁₁₉

thursday
30   ₁₂₀

friday
☽ 1   ₁₂₁

saturday
2   ₁₂₂

sunday
3   ₁₂₃

s	m	t	w	t	f	s
					1	2
3	4	5	6	7	8	9
10	11	12	13	14	15	16
17	18	19	20	21	22	23
24	25	26	27	28	29	30
31						

MAY

The New York Times

BY RANDOLPH ROSS / EDITED BY WILL SHORTZ / 10-09-05

ACROSS

1 A pinch, maybe
6 Provide food for many
11 Some dance records, for short
14 Musical Young
18 Snouted animal
19 Of service
20 Double-crosser
21 "Lay it ___!"
22 1996 Helen Fielding book made into a film starring Renée Zellweger
25 Assault with a grenade, as a commanding officer
26 Move, quickly
27 Space chimp of 1961
28 Memo abbr.
29 Olympic rings, e.g.
30 Absorb the cost of
31 Suffix with social
32 Best-selling 2003 Alice Sebold novel
36 Three of ___
38 Capital of Hubei province
40 Israel's Weizman
41 1995 Ellen DeGeneres best seller
48 Very pleasant
49 Like some translations
50 Alternative to oil
53 Larry McMurtry novel made into an Emmy-winning TV series
57 Pharmaceutical giant
58 Longoria of "Desperate Housewives"
59 A thief might take one
60 Salad ingredient
62 Part
63 Not clerical
64 Battle reminder
65 2003 Bill O'Reilly political best seller
70 "Christ of St. John of the Cross" artist
71 "Wheel of Fortune" request
72 Bad party guest
73 Kennel cry
74 Made up one's mind about
75 Grazing spot
76 Imperiled
79 1994 semi-autobiographical novel by Anna Quindlen
83 Son of Prince Valiant
84 Heroic deeds
86 Monopoly maker
87 1939 Agatha Christie classic
92 Pakistani tongue
94 Early American diplomat Silas
95 Nine: Prefix
96 1929 Virginia Woolf title
101 Place for a team's insignia
103 Atlantic catch
104 Winter Palace resident
105 Sibilant talk
106 Dr. Pavlov
108 Author Jaffe
109 Stay too long on the beach
110 2000 essay collection by David Sedaris
115 Protected, at sea
116 Before
117 They give people big heads
118 Key
119 Sale site
120 Filch
121 Lilac, e.g.
122 Bonnie's beau

DOWN

1 Like poorly washed windows
2 Something a maid might break
3 Many a prom coif
4 Cookie fruit
5 Springs
6 Stephen King canine
7 Squares things
8 "___ the season ..."
9 Trains in Chicago
10 Signal to stop
11 Poet's inspiration
12 Last of a Monday-to-Friday series
13 "Let It Snow, Let It Snow, Let It Snow" composer
14 Restricted area
15 Dress
16 "This looks verrry bad for me!"
17 Kids' blocks
22 Silver-scaled fish
23 Big bang cause
24 Suffix with proverb
31 Subject in foreign language class
32 Sem. degree
33 Applaud
34 "The ___ near"
35 Actress Sobieski
37 "Uh-uh!"
38 Baylor's home
39 Odd
42 Pilot's dir.
43 Rx instruction
44 Capri suffix
45 George of "La Cage aux Folles"

May

s	m	t	w	t	f	s
					1	2
3	4	5	6	7	8	9
10	11	12	13	14	15	16
17	18	19	20	21	22	23
24	25	26	27	28	29	30
31						

MAY

BANK HOLIDAY (UK)   *monday*

9 AM   Dr Bruce

4 124

CINCO DE MAYO   *tuesday*

5 125

wednesday

6 126

thursday

7 127

friday

8 128

saturday

9 129

MOTHER'S DAY   *sunday*

10 130

The New York Times

112 Blue, perhaps
114 Romeo or Juliet
115 Aging Nintendo icon?
118 Football stat.
119 Newton, e.g.
120 Went smoothly
121 ___ being
122 Some batteries
123 Domain of the goddess Tethys
124 Go above and beyond
125 Perfect, e.g.

DOWN

1 City in 84-Down
2 Whence the line "The True North strong and free"
3 Can opener
4 Women of Paris
5 Purposely try to lose
6 Mercury or Saturn
7 Put in order
8 Brown family member
9 Puppeteer Tony
10 Collegiate Bulldog
11 Where some think monsters live
12 Rubberneck
13 Waiting
14 It can be thrown from a horse
15 Let have it
16 Optometrist's concern
17 Some museum displays
18 Overrun
24 Souvenir buy
26 "You're crushing the watch!"?
30 Itsy-bitsy
33 Oscar winner Benigni
34 "That was bad"
37 Camera attachment, informally
38 Happy ___
39 Pond plant
40 Pompon waver's cry
41 Crypt cover
44 Gas pump's place?
47 Moon of Uranus
49 Gentlemen they're not
50 Regarding
52 Star of "Scared to Death," 1947
53 Men and women
54 One that "eats shoots and leaves"
55 Encourage
56 Animal catcher
58 2000 Renée Zellweger title role

BY KYLE MAHOWALD / EDITED BY WILL SHORTZ / 10-16-05

ACROSS

1 Was in a blue state
6 "Hold on!"
12 "You go, ___!"
16 Dr.'s order
19 Eyes?
20 Infrequent political event
21 1998 Sarah McLachlan hit
22 Asian capital
23 Spanish dancers' residence?
25 Hit the links
27 Shore sights
28 Jerk
29 Honey
31 Chin-ups and pull-ups develop them
32 Charlemagne's domain: Abbr.
34 ___ time
35 Monkey business
36 Author LeShan
37 Israeli leaders?
42 Words to a bride and groom
43 Take in
45 Lodge fellows
46 Removed
48 Shopper's aid
50 Captain of literature
51 To-do
55 Not close gently
57 Big name in antacids
60 Island settled by shipwrecked colonists in 1609
62 Run-in
63 Classic sports car
64 Old-fashioned education
66 Zapper
67 Sniffler's keepsake?
72 Melodious
73 Astin of "Lord of the Rings"
74 Keep out
75 Aid in solving the disappearance of the Thin Man
76 Car dealers' offerings
78 Member of a blended family
81 Trident-shaped letters
82 One side of a debate
83 Some tax advisers, for short
85 Danger for sailors
87 Symbol of strength
89 Movie roll
91 Go in all directions
94 ___-American
97 Photogenic cats?
100 Lush
102 Snaky swimmers
104 Lines of praise
105 Suffix with tank
106 Bygone royal
107 Square
110 Danger for sailors

May

monday
11 131

tuesday
12 132

wednesday
13 133

thursday
14 134

friday
15 135

ARMED FORCES DAY

saturday
16 136

sunday
☾ 17 137

s	m	t	w	t	f	s
					1	2
3	4	5	6	7	8	9
10	11	12	13	14	15	16
17	18	19	20	21	22	23
24	25	26	27	28	29	30
31						

MAY

BY CON PEDERSON / EDITED BY WILL SHORTZ / 10-23-05

ACROSS

1 "Meet John Doe" director
6 Wooden shoe
11 PIN spotters?
15 Realize
19 Weaving willow
20 Softly
21 Bigmouth
22 Relieve
23 Dullish
24 Layabout
25 Poor actor staying sober?
27 "Yeah, we've got that," e.g.?
30 Aligned
31 Longtime "Today" co-host
32 Olin of "Chocolat"
34 ___-Magnon
35 Philosophy of the "Chuang Tzu"
38 Extra-base hit, probably?
44 Solo
45 Et ___
48 Like tea
49 F.D.R.'s wiring program
50 Doesn't own
52 Fancy home features
55 ___ powers
56 Now it's Thailand
57 Review of fall fashion accessories?
61 Skate part
62 Ticket
63 Astrological point
64 Trawlers' nets
65 Fetter
69 Sat
70 Agitation
71 Humiliates
72 Decision points
73 First name in court fiction
74 Official denial
75 Excused from saving a sinking boat?
81 "Casablanca" role
82 Obscured
83 Having nothing obscured
84 Balderdash
85 Like
86 Given to glad-handing
89 Double-bonded compound
91 Not forgetting
92 Fouled in basketball, in a way?
96 Prayer
98 Undisguised
99 Pianist/composer Dohnányi
100 Beau
102 Barren
107 Fake molding in a room?
112 Guidebook for golf greens?
114 Mideast potentate
115 Butterfly in youth
116 No, to Natasha
117 Make a long story short?
118 Like fur coats
119 City north of Cologne
120 Familiar truths
121 Try again
122 Rectangular paving stones
123 Was very bright

DOWN

1 Italian silk center
2 Wise ___ owl
3 Tropical helmet material
4 Practice tit for tat
5 Venues
6 Skyline pointer
7 Ambulance attendant, often
8 Aloe, naturally
9 Low tie
10 P.G.A. Tour site, ___ Pines
11 Oberhausen cry
12 Catch-22
13 Where "Guernica" was hung during W.W. II
14 Day in a heat wave
15 Run again
16 Tupper of Tupperware fame
17 Start of a sowing adage
18 Leave in a hurry, with "out"
26 Got along
28 Russian assembly
29 Channel changer
33 Part of the Old World: Abbr.
35 Tongue-curling
36 Blueprint datum
37 Farm sound
38 Can
39 Decreasing numbers of
40 It's in the past
41 European launch vehicle
42 Hard to lift
43 Most contrived
46 Drink from a machine
47 Spillane's "___ Jury"
51 Game with a yellow card
53 Skip
54 Dweller on Cape Prince of Wales
56 Insignificant
58 1912 Physics Nobelist ___ Dalen
59 Site of a historic 1905 revolt

May

VICTORIA DAY (CANADA)

monday
18 138

tuesday
19 139

wednesday
20 140

thursday
21 141

friday
22 142

saturday
23 143

sunday
24 144

s	m	t	w	t	f	s
					1	2
3	4	5	6	7	8	9
10	11	12	13	14	15	16
17	18	19	20	21	22	23
24	25	26	27	28	29	30
31						

22. FIELD OF DREAMS

The New York Times

BY DAVID J. KAHN / EDITED BY WILL SHORTZ / 10-30-05

ACROSS

1 Recovers, with "up"
7 Delibes opera
12 Wrinkle, maybe
19 Noted support group
20 Gibson garnish
21 Caffeine source: Var.
22 A man goes for a walk and …
25 Bird: Prefix
26 "Let's not go there"
27 Mother of Pollux and Helen
28 ___ cheese
30 Break
32 Like Bruckner's Symphony No. 7
33 Upper hand
36 Activists
37 When he pops the cork, a genie appears and says, "…"
43 2004 biopic that was a Best Picture nominee
44 Pronunciation difficulty
45 Like the sugar in cotton candy
46 Piedmont wine city
48 Lorelei Lee's creator
50 Have a hunch
51 Some health info ads, for short
55 The man says, "I want to see …"
60 Kind of leather
61 Fighting Tigers' sch.
62 John
63 Totaled
64 2003 Will Ferrell title role
65 He then hands the genie …
71 Springy steps
72 It's measured by the meter
74 Big-league
75 Scoundrel
76 One who's out of touch
77 The genie studies it for a while and finally says, "This is impossible. So …"
84 ZIP code 10001 locale: Abbr.
85 Radiation units
86 Above, in Aachen
87 Support, in a way
88 Composer ___ Carlo Menotti
89 Rye alternative
91 Fretted strings
92 The man says, "I always wanted to see …"
102 See 50-Down
103 Starting
104 "Sweet!"
105 Go bonkers
106 "Three Sisters" sister
107 Exertion
110 Grab some chow?
113 "The Waste Land" monogram
114 The genie replies, "…"
119 See 94-Down
120 Double order, perhaps
121 Conjured up
122 Some terriers
123 Jones of the Miracle Mets
124 Scares off

DOWN

1 Bush activity
2 Big Turkish export
3 Outlaw
4 Put a stopper on
5 "Mahogany" star, 1975
6 How some rivers proceed
7 Sewing machine gizmo
8 Con
9 Coyly playful
10 Small particle: Abbr.
11 Dir. of I-64 going up Ky.
12 Tough problem to face?
13 Push
14 Noted exile site
15 Papua New Guinea port
16 How shoelaces are often tied
17 Central parts
18 Bygone numbers
23 Cherry variety
24 Spread out on a table?
29 Seat, slangily
31 Highlander pattern
34 Sot's problem
35 Swindle
36 Remote location
38 Like some church matters
39 Stacks
40 Brought into play
41 Kind of column
42 Invalid
46 Fight stopper
47 Branching marine growth
48 Phoebe's player on "Friends"
49 "Movin' ___"
50 With 102-Across, London-New York time difference
51 ___-green
52 City in a 1968 Dionne Warwick top 10 hit
53 Comparably tense
54 Smelly smoke
56 Popular street name
57 John of England
58 ___-jongg

May

MEMORIAL DAY
BANK HOLIDAY (UK)

monday
25 145

tuesday
26 146

wednesday
27 147

thursday
28 148

friday
29 149

saturday
30 150

sunday
31 151

s	m	t	w	t	f	s
					1	2
3	4	5	6	7	8	9
10	11	12	13	14	15	16
17	18	19	20	21	22	23
24	25	26	27	28	29	30
31						

MAY

The New York Times

BY MAXWELL H. D. JOHNSON JR. / EDITED BY WILL SHORTZ / 11-06-05

ACROSS

1 Act high-handedly?
7 Kind of film
11 Having gone through a flood, say
17 Opposite of away
19 Boxers alternative
22 Neaten (up)
23 Sudden shock?
25 Precise
26 Abstain
27 1910's film star known as The Vamp
28 Interdicts
30 Père's frère
31 Farmer's prayer
33 "Batman" fight scene word
34 Book after Ezra: Abbr.
35 Durango domicile
39 Halloween expense?
43 French concern: Abbr.
46 Recreating
48 Beethoven dedicatee
49 Curious one
51 Creepy neighborhood?
54 Bobbing for apples, e.g.
55 Watchmaker's sci.
56 Weight lifters' units
57 Not only that
59 Laughing matter
60 Indecipherable
62 Onetime home of Kit Carson
63 Knows about
65 Apparition on a "Concentration" board?
69 Philatelic design on an envelope
73 Bats
74 Shouted encouragement
79 Tuning note instrument
80 Iris holder
81 College QB, maybe
83 1998 BP purchase
84 Prop for Quasimodo
87 Study of ghouls and goblins?
89 Grandmotherly type
90 Angler with pots
92 Provocation, metaphorically
93 ___ Halles, old Parisian market
94 Tuneup for a Halloween conveyance?
98 Spanish direction
99 Alphabetic trio
101 Grab ___
102 Puts
104 Sponge mushroom
106 Italian painter Guido
107 Poker declaration
109 Architectural projections
114 Singer of the aria "Dio! mi potevi scagliar"
116 Periodic Halloween sight?

119 Ahab, for one
120 Computer letters
121 Long green
122 Bedouins and Tuaregs
123 Future atty.'s hurdle
124 Made a haunted house sound

DOWN

1 Public relations effort
2 River of Tuscany
3 Riga native
4 Not mint
5 114-Across, e.g.
6 Recent U.S.N.A. grad
7 Good buddy
8 Astronomical bear
9 M.D.'s requirement
10 Brewers' needs
11 Worrying sound to a balloonist
12 Other side
13 Military reconnaissance tool
14 Group of cacklers in wooden shoes?
15 Biol. branch
16 Protected state bird
18 It's found above the ankle
20 Cold drink
21 What to call the barber of Seville
24 Airport shuttles
29 Cops
32 Tan and others
33 Work with needles
35 Kid's Halloween candy, e.g.
36 One of a French trio
37 Vice president before Gerald
38 Give out
40 Maintain
41 Parts of la Polynésie
42 Receptacle for some Halloween contributions
44 "___ my case"
45 Have an ___ the ground
47 Maintain
50 Martial arts place
52 Barbershop request
53 Not kick off
54 Land-clearing device
57 Nail site
58 Explorer's need
61 Snitch
62 Best
63 Neighbor of Jor.
64 Attack by plane, in a way
66 Jacksonville-to-Daytona Beach dir.

June

monday

1 152

tuesday

2 153

wednesday

3 154

thursday

4 155

friday

5 156

saturday

6 157

sunday

7 158

s	m	t	w	t	f	s
	1	2	3	4	5	6
7	8	9	10	11	12	13
14	15	16	17	18	19	20
21	22	23	24	25	26	27
28	29	30				

The New York Times

BY ELIZABETH C. GORSKI / EDITED BY WILL SHORTZ / 11-13-05

ACROSS

1 Scientific research center
7 Belittling sort
11 Bills, e.g.
15 Two of fifty
18 Brush aside
19 Feeling
20 Italian province or its capital
21 Sharp-penned Maureen
23 Strong-arm
24 "___ Apart," 2003 Vin Diesel flick
25 Low in fat
26 Person seen in court
27 Free service started in 1905
31 Nobel Prize subj.
32 AT&T acquisition of 1991
33 Travel between the poles?
34 Irving Berlin's "___ a Piano"
35 Calendar abbr.
36 Popular 1970's-80's vocal-harmony quartet
42 1930's-50's actor J. ___ Naish
44 Nastase of tennis
45 Cross
46 Is beholden to
48 Reacts to, as a joke
51 More than exasperation
54 1993 Robert De Niro film
59 Military joes
60 The Supreme Court, e.g.
63 Snorkler's interest
64 First prize at the 1992 Olympics
65 One who's an -ologist, maybe
66 Major industry of Madeira
67 What thousands do on the first Sunday of every November
72 Best way to drive
73 Do some carbo-loading, e.g.
74 Printer problem
75 Bird call
76 Best, as advice
77 Furtive
78 Teens with tiaras
81 Laugh sound
82 "C'est magnifique!"
85 "___ cost you!"
86 Ingredient in Cookies 'n Cream ice cream
87 Bowed, in music
90 Fixes up, as a ship
94 What people follow when they 67-Across
101 Turndowns
102 Month in Madrid
103 Nancy Drew's guy
104 Advanced degree
105 Bern's river
106 Classic best seller by Betty Smith
113 Bullwinkle, for one
114 1890's veep ___ P. Morton
115 "David Copperfield" wife
116 Sight from Turkey
118 ___-Soviet relations
119 Goons
120 Opposin'
121 Works with the hands
122 Shooting marble
123 Ready to come out of the 109-Down
124 Boxer's punch
125 Regret

DOWN

1 Lighter handle?
2 Prankster's cry
3 TV drama length
4 "Two Women" Oscar winner
5 Musical ties, essentially
6 ___ greens
7 Big name in ad agencies
8 I, for one
9 North African port
10 It can be found step by step
11 Talk radio feature
12 Between ports
13 "South Park" boy
14 Female deer
15 Collectible Fords
16 :56, timewise
17 Try to avoid hitting
22 Place for a tumbler
28 Politico Richards
29 Calypso kin
30 Fivers
31 Mail Boxes ___
36 Cut
37 1959 Wimbledon winner ___ Olmedo
38 Buster Brown's dog
39 Turn's partner
40 Translation material
41 Not your ordinary film director
43 Beam at the very top of a house
47 Expressionless
49 Operatic prince
50 Cable channel for kids
51 Apart from others
52 Work on more, as a farrier might
53 Irish runner Coghlan
54 Ornate wall hanging

June

monday

8 159

tuesday

9 160

wednesday

10 161

thursday

11 162

friday

12 163

saturday

13 164

s	m	t	w	t	f	s
	1	2	3	4	5	6
7	8	9	10	11	12	13
14	15	16	17	18	19	20
21	22	23	24	25	26	27
28	29	30				

FLAG DAY

sunday

14 165

BY BRENDAN EMMETT QUIGLEY / EDITED BY WILL SHORTZ / 11-20-05

ACROSS

1 "A Passage to India" actor, 1984
9 Cultivation
16 Game divs.
20 Water, colloquially
21 They haven't any definite forms
22 Cover up
23 The SS Manhattan was the first commercial ship to cross it
25 Rain collector
26 N.Y.C. subway line
27 It may precede a nickname
28 Buenos ___
29 "Hooray for Love" composer
30 Scrap
32 Post-9/11 slogan
36 Take down the aisle again
38 Big name in Fox News
39 Made sport of
42 The Father of English History
45 Historic town on the Vire
46 "___ Cried" (1962 hit)
49 Place to get links
50 Macaroni dish with ground beef and a little tomato sauce
55 Come together
56 Neuter
57 After-dinner drink
58 Sculptor James ___ Fraser
59 Get a sense something's up
62 Doesn't just throw off
66 Engine measures: Abbr.
67 Warm winter wear
70 Novelist O'Flaherty
72 Anorexic's aversion
73 Stealthy activity
76 They get pins and needles
78 Do
80 Depilatory brand
81 "Your point being …?"
82 Entertainer accompanying a slide guitar and harmonica, maybe
87 Son of Leah
88 10 cc, e.g.
89 Something that may be on a house
90 "Star Trek: T.N.G." counselor
91 Actor Quinn
92 Palestinian nationalist group
95 Ear inflammation
98 1977 Toni Morrison novel
103 Jim Backus provided his voice
107 U-shaped piece of wood
108 "Uncle Vanya" woman
109 18-Down writer
110 Coastal flier
111 Baloney peddler
112 Earthquake cause
117 Concert halls
118 Malleable
119 Utterly lost
120 Withered
121 Operatic tenor ___ Alagna
122 Place to stretch

DOWN

1 Arlo's partner in the comics
2 Festoon
3 Radio ___, broadcasting service to Cuba
4 One with a time-sensitive job, for short
5 Like some hooks
6 Guy from England
7 Soap ingredient
8 Marks (out)
9 Golf gimme
10 Japanese porcelain
11 Get crushed by
12 Minor
13 Court org.
14 Skit part
15 A foot wide?
16 Kind of keyboard
17 Refrain part, perhaps
18 See 109-Across, with "The"
19 Devote, as time
24 Overdrawn?
29 Pitched
31 Feed facts to, maybe
33 Family tree listing: Abbr.
34 Plus
35 Greenwich greeting
37 Temporarily suspended
39 Spirited dances
40 "Your slip is showing"
41 Bar challenge
43 Decline
44 Green
46 "Is that what you expected?"
47 Command position
48 Surveys
50 Take ___ from (copy)
51 1957 song that begins "The most beautiful sound I ever heard …"
52 Seed covering
53 Underground experiment, for short
54 Eastern wrap
56 Camera inits.
60 Cap

June

monday
15 166

tuesday
16 167

wednesday
17 168

thursday
18 169

friday
19 170

saturday
20 171

FATHER'S DAY
SUMMER SOLSTICE 05:45 UTC

sunday
21 172

s	m	t	w	t	f	s
	1	2	3	4	5	6
7	8	9	10	11	12	13
14	15	16	17	18	19	20
21	22	23	24	25	26	27
28	29	30				

26. BLUE STREAK

By Harvey Estes and Nancy Salomon / Edited by Will Shortz / 11-21-04

ACROSS

1 Special team
6 Chi-town paper
10 Get lost
15 Dumptruckful
19 "Twelfth Night" role
20 Mrs. Chaplin
21 "Ta-da!"
22 Word processor command
23 March trailer
24 Haltingly
26 Kind of bike
27 Used up
28 Space flight's starting point
29 Nice-smelling gifts
30 Rhode Island's motto
31 Colored a bit
33 Shake
34 Rights of passage, e.g.
36 Cook's exhortation
38 McCartney title
40 Despot of yore
41 Portion of a ton: Abbr.
44 Aerosol output
45 Hems and haws
46 Totaled
50 Agreeable
52 F.D.R. power project
53 Made book marks?
56 Extra cost in mail order
57 Choler
58 Fights dirty, in a way
59 Martinique, e.g.
60 Street of mystery
61 Pro pitchers
63 Rod attachment
64 Some votes
65 Mock plea for civil language
69 Mix up
70 Came to
71 Pricey
72 Cut
74 Russert of "Meet the Press"
75 Needed a doctor
76 Stale
77 Scarface portrayer
78 Like some income
80 South-of-the-border shout
81 Got a slice of
83 Obscure
84 Comic Gilliam
85 "Rush Hour" star, 1998
86 Heartbeat, so to speak
87 Abbey ___
90 Fortune 500 inits.
91 Invoice word
93 Coin of the realm
97 Sewed up
99 Perfumes with a joss stick
104 Open
105 First child

[continued clues]

106 Waxed bombastic
108 Supermodel Campbell
109 Slave of opera
110 That, to this
112 Values on a scale of 0 to 100
113 Ship part
114 60-Across's boss
115 It's not good
116 Ties up
117 Highlands tongue
118 Plain writing
119 Hawk
120 "I Am Woman" singer, 1972

DOWN

1 "Cease" at sea
2 Painter Fra Filippo ___
3 "Two Women" Oscar winner
4 Black bird
5 Stored (away)
6 Words before and after "or not"
7 King's champion
8 Ahead
9 Puts on the hook?
10 Elm and Peachtree: Abbr.
11 Ship provisioners
12 Roadside pull-off
13 Oil worker
14 Imbroglios
15 Like Wittenberg University in Ohio
16 Continuously
17 Crack
18 Some stadium features
25 Best-selling 1974 detective novel
32 Yankee nickname of old
35 Niles's ex on "Frasier"
37 Cry at the card table
39 Investment option, briefly
41 Under the table
42 Serendipitous
43 Make fit
47 All over
48 Looking good on the tube
49 Lyrical lines
50 High degree
51 Clothes closer
52 Something good
53 Saturday night special
54 Truly enjoyed
55 Firms
57 Penned up
58 Like cattle on the range
61 Burn ___ in one's pocket
62 Faked out, in the rink

monday
22   173

tuesday
23   174

wednesday
24   175

thursday
25   176

friday
26   177

saturday
27   178

s	m	t	w	t	f	s
	1	2	3	4	5	6
7	8	9	10	11	12	13
14	15	16	17	18	19	20
21	22	23	24	25	26	27
28	29	30				

sunday
28   179

27. REJECTED COLLEGE MASCOTS

The New York Times

BY PATRICK MERRELL / EDITED BY WILL SHORTZ / 11-27-05

ACROSS

1 Crows
6 "A Passage to India" character
11 Popular player since 2001
15 Kids
20 Baker, of a sort
21 Bulb unit
22 Exclusive of anything else
23 Author Sinclair
24 Of last month
25 Incarnation
27 Best-selling Hasbro toy introduced in the 1960's
28 Mascot #1
31 Seafood selection
32 Feeling
33 It might make the torso seem moreso
34 Hypo meas.
35 One taking advantage of a long arm
37 Q.E.D. part
38 Ka ___ (Hawaii's South Cape)
40 Former German president Johannes ___
41 Duel personalities?
42 G.P.S. heading
43 Off-land lander
47 Gray head?
50 Lights (into)
51 Mascot #2
54 Rising times
57 Things best let be, proverbially
60 Symbols used in Navajo and Mayan art
62 Nut
63 Heavy
64 Barracks locale
66 "In excelsis ___"
67 Mail-sorting ctr.
69 Genetic inits.
70 Mr. Hulot's player, in films
71 Galoot-like
73 Street coat?
75 Mascot #3
81 Name-callers, maybe
84 One of 12 tiles in mah-jongg
85 Existence, to Claudius
89 Eight-time Norris Trophy winner
90 First thing Iowa State cheerleaders ask for?
91 It used to be pitched
94 Uffizi display
95 Best of the best
97 Landlocked land
99 Rising
102 Agog
103 Writer Carroll
105 Mascot #4
108 Theo. Roosevelt Natl. Park site
110 End in the Bible?
111 Shell carrier
112 CD burners
115 Tagged
118 Country singer Joe
120 QB's gains
121 Show appreciation
122 Acquisitive sort
123 Mideast org.
124 Scrap
126 Petach Tikva resident
129 Armory grp.
130 Mascot #5
134 1960's TV actress Stevens
136 Tries to trap something
137 One rolling with the Stones?
138 Skilled
139 "Smooth Operator" singer
140 Win by ___
141 Mooring spots
142 Clipped
143 List abbr.
144 Forlorn one
145 Union general

DOWN

1 Swindlers
2 Laser surgery targets
3 In the center of
4 Kind of ray
5 Hardly one of hoi polloi
6 "Hard ___!" (nautical order)
7 Airhead
8 Imprison
9 Hotelier Helmsley
10 Bandleader's start
11 Neat as a pin
12 Henhouse sounds
13 Caen's river
14 Prevents
15 Corked vessel
16 Like George Washington's church
17 Mascot #6
18 Decorated, as leather
19 Bad looks
20 Kitties
26 No fan of Pizarro, certainly
29 Devices in electrical networks
30 Act the ogler
36 Burn cause
39 Urgent transmission, for short
40 Country star's sitcom
43 Compos mentis
44 Roulette bet
45 2000 Olympics host
46 Most up-to-date
48 Basso Pinza
49 Startled interjection
51 "Sorry, Charlie!"
52 Narc's haul
53 Sweater style
55 A doofus might do it
56 It makes clothes close
57 Short order in a diner
58 Voice vote
59 Rod
61 Springs
64 Farm calls
65 Rear

Jun/Jul

monday 🌙 **29** 180

tuesday **30** 181

CANADA DAY (CANADA) *wednesday* **1** 182

thursday **2** 183

INDEPENDENCE DAY OBSERVED *friday* **3** 184

INDEPENDENCE DAY *saturday* **4** 185

sunday **5** 186

s	m	t	w	t	f	s
			1	2	3	4
5	6	7	8	9	10	11
12	13	14	15	16	17	18
19	20	21	22	23	24	25
26	27	28	29	30	31	

JULY

The New York Times

BY PETER ABIDE / EDITED BY WILL SHORTZ / 12-04-05

ACROSS

1 Peter ___
7 Awakens
14 Hot coffee hazard
19 Queen of mystery
20 Bits of shells
21 Advice-giving sort
22 One who may give you fits
23 Upper crust of the N.B.A.?
25 Mideast capital
26 They may carry antibodies
27 Cold one
28 "Hot" one
29 One cautioning about opening a soda can?
33 Made heroic
35 Sports stat
36 "You don't say!"
38 Big lug
39 Antlered animal of the Old World
42 Mail-in for a toy ninja?
48 "___ Little Girl," Shirley Temple film
49 Football officials, slangily
52 Makes even
53 Wine holder
54 As ___ resort
57 Prefix with reading
58 Borden who founded the Borden Co.
59 High-performance Camaro
60 One who opts for a convertible?
64 Thrown together
67 Fast Eddie's girlfriend in "The Hustler"
68 Prefix with centric
70 It has a nut on each end
71 Tossed
74 Playwright in rare form?
78 About
79 Pronoun with "somme"
81 Symbols used in angle measurement
82 Jim Henson gave him voice
83 "Fantasy Island" prop
84 Plaintiffs
86 Order member since 1534
89 Baseball C.E.O.'s
90 Part of Santa's team on a computer?
93 Papal court
96 Scrap for Rover
97 I.R.S. worker: Abbr.
98 Future ferns
100 Hot dog
105 Waikiki ringmaster?
110 Afghan makeup
111 Tennyson work
113 Sound heard through a stethoscope
114 Tools with teeth
115 Miss Road Pavement?
119 Hocked
120 ___ ease
121 "Star Trek" directive
122 Handles
123 Villainous looks
124 Serious scoldings
125 Furthest out there

DOWN

1 Draw on again
2 Budget rival
3 It's often seen over a bowl
4 After the fact
5 Magnetite, for one
6 Norse god of war
7 Cricket sounds
8 Club publication
9 ___-jongg
10 Capable, jocularly
11 "Superior" one
12 Dakota dwelling
13 The ___ twins of "New York Minute," 2004
14 League for L.S.U. and Mississippi St.
15 Socialite wannabe
16 "You've got ___!"
17 "I'll help!"
18 Woods nymph
20 Wind phenomenon
24 Baroque
26 Talked a blue streak?
30 W, for one
31 They may clash among titans
32 Mardi Gras royal
34 Work
37 Kett of the comics
39 Den din
40 Faulkner's femme fatale ___ Varner
41 Rubber-burning area
42 Jazz scores
43 "___ my flesh of brass?": Job
44 Bar exercise
45 Important info for advertisers
46 Mekong River locale
47 Delineate
50 Ascap alternative
51 On easy street
55 It may be fixed
56 Famous Amos
58 Vise
59 Slugabed
61 Shock absorber
62 Dropped a dime, so to speak
63 Judge in I Samuel

July

monday

6 187

tuesday

○ **7** 188

wednesday

8 189

thursday

9 190

friday

10 191

saturday

11 192

sunday

12 193

s	m	t	w	t	f	s
			1	2	3	4
5	6	7	8	9	10	11
12	13	14	15	16	17	18
19	20	21	22	23	24	25
26	27	28	29	30	31	

The New York Times

BY HAL TURNER / EDITED BY WILL SHORTZ / 01-02-04

ACROSS

1 Novelist known for "locked-room" mysteries
5 Just about hopeless
10 Former first lady's name
14 Rash problem
18 Potpourri
19 Terra firma
20 Coleridge's "___ Khan"
21 "A Doll's House" heroine
22 Long-running column
25 Hostage crisis group
26 Those reversing
27 Pungent
28 What's happening
30 Major or Thatcher, e.g.
31 French department
32 Cool
33 Nook
36 "In Search Of ..." host
37 At sixes and sevens
41 "The Wreck of the Mary ___"
42 Cafeteria
44 James Clavell best seller "___-Pan"
45 Stops up
46 Co. V.I.P.
47 Like most of Oman
48 Glossary entry
49 Dubious "gift"
50 Hammer wielder
54 Things put on houses
55 Manage
57 Leigh Hunt's "About Ben ___"
58 Derrières
59 Newspaper department
60 Funny Mike
61 Portobello alternative
62 Toiletry item
63 "I Believe" singer, 1953
64 Islets of Langerhans locale
67 Fugitive's creation
68 L-shaped tool
70 "I'm Real" singer's nickname
71 It's half the faun
72 Twinge
73 Modern ice cream flavor
74 Keyboard section
75 Common test subject
76 Classic doll
80 Have a cow
81 Letter wearers, e.g.
83 Find new tenants for
84 Spends pleasantly, with "away"
85 Kadett maker
86 Calls, old-style
87 Hue close to aqua
88 Video store category
91 Video store category
92 Like ocher
96 Lug
97 When some people pick up turkeys
100 Saying nothing
101 Bridge seats
102 Make beam
103 Lawn-Boy alternative
104 Pony provoker
105 Tango moves
106 Struck out
107 Crimson rivals

DOWN

1 Harry who co-founded Columbia Pictures
2 Live ___ (be someone you're not)
3 Arboreal age indicator
4 Some muscles
5 In the presence of
6 Bird making a basket
7 The libido, in psychiatry
8 Balance provider
9 Head of Iran beginning 1997
10 Shoplifter's giveaway, perhaps
11 Bidding site
12 Camera type, briefly
13 Blue
14 As originally arranged
15 Country partner?
16 Mountaineer's challenge
17 Tops
20 Popular saxophonist
23 Boiling point?
24 Captain of industry
29 Bozos
31 Belarus's capital
32 Away
33 Puff ___
34 Car dealer's offering
35 Popular negotiation location
36 Flower girl, sometimes
37 Billiards bounce
38 Worker who shouldn't have acrophobia
39 Makes
40 Makes indistinct
42 Mild oaths
43 Refreshing spots
46 Surveyors' maps
48 Microwave feature
50 Felicity
51 Entrance
52 Places of 50-Down
53 Cousin of a mole
54 Clumsy move
56 Lusitania sinker
58 Big name in infomercials

July

BANK HOLIDAY (N. IRELAND)

monday

13 194

tuesday

14 195

wednesday

☾ **15** 196

thursday

16 197

friday

17 198

saturday

18 199

sunday

19 200

s	m	t	w	t	f	s
			1	2	3	4
5	6	7	8	9	10	11
12	13	14	15	16	17	18
19	20	21	22	23	24	25
26	27	28	29	30	31	

The New York Times

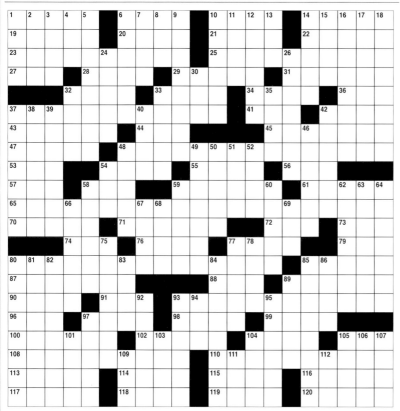

BY MANNY NOSOWSKY / EDITED BY WILL SHORTZ / 10-24-04

ACROSS

1 More than high
6 Page
10 Russian name meaning "holy"
14 Lord's workers
19 Where the lion spared Androcles
20 Transition in logic
21 Godsend
22 Somewhat, after "of"
23 Laird or thane?
25 Ex-Dallas coach's daytime show?
27 Sweetie
28 Additionally
29 Web mag
31 Cultural breakdown
32 Blackthorn
33 Word with beetle or movie
34 "What, again?!"
36 Denver summer hrs.
37 Diamond cutter's pace?
41 –: Abbr.
42 What traffic cones may show
43 Ear malady
44 "Thimble Theater" name
45 Spinner
47 Girl in "The Gondoliers"
48 Iciness and wetness?
53 Rap's Dr. ___
54 Loads of
55 First name in fashion
56 Working out well?
57 "Bed-in" participant, 1969
58 Traveler's aid
59 Prioritizing by army medics, e.g.
61 Benevolent witchcraft
65 What Wordsworth did before he got hip?
70 Giants on the sports page
71 Liking a lot
72 Bronze metal
73 Bite for a bark beetle
74 Prefix with metric
76 Do
77 Tiptop
79 A caliph of Islam
80 Games, games and more games?
85 One in a booth, maybe
87 In pigtails, e.g.
88 Wrongdoing
89 Bridge problem
90 Exhibition area
91 Dirt disher ___ Smith
93 Why water got diverted in the garden?
96 Newsman Bradley and others
97 Quick note
98 Results of a wrong turn, perhaps
99 Tidy up, in a way
100 Falling star
102 It may be cradled
104 Like one smitten
105 Answer sheet
108 Nickname for a pushy priest?
110 Young female marchers?
113 Skin ailment
114 Fictional Jane
115 ___ Sea (inland body of water)
116 Milking a cow, e.g.
117 Lavender, for one
118 Set foot (on)
119 Park Ave. address part
120 Banana oil, e.g.

DOWN

1 Flirt, in old slang
2 It's a gas
3 It's a gas
4 Quarterback's error: Abbr.
5 Alabama's state flower
6 Not so great
7 One-named artist
8 Gray
9 Prophesied
10 Require
11 Part of F.S.L.I.C.
12 Liking a lot
13 "Then what?"
14 Decline
15 "The sign of extra service" sloganeer, once
16 School pal, maybe
17 "Sorry, no can do"
18 Workplace for Michelangelo
24 "A Lesson From ___"
26 Ended a call in London
30 More than daze
32 Goes down
33 How to palm a card
35 Mainz mister
37 Note
38 God, with "the"
39 Sage
40 In next to no time
42 Obtained from milk
46 Oolong tea exporter
48 Karel ___, writer who coined the word "robot"
49 Stopped working, as medicine
50 Native's opposite
51 Relative of a mallard
52 Like brioche
54 Natl. Nutrition Mo.
58 Abbr. in a salutation

July

monday
20 201

tuesday
21 202

wednesday
22 203

thursday
23 204

friday
24 205

saturday
25 206

sunday
26 207

s	m	t	w	t	f	s
			1	2	3	4
5	6	7	8	9	10	11
12	13	14	15	16	17	18
19	20	21	22	23	24	25
26	27	28	29	30	31	

31. THE REFEREE OF ROMANCE

The New York Times

BY PATRICK BERRY / EDITED BY WILL SHORTZ / 10-31-04

ACROSS

1 Went down to second?
5 Did laps
9 Place for table umbrellas
13 Like oxfords
18 Common Web site link
19 ___ Minor
20 Famous mausoleum site
21 Powdered soap brand
22 Locket shape
23 Friend barges in while gent is making amorous overtures; ref declares …
26 ___ Hold'em (poker variant)
28 R & B singer Bryson
29 Two-time loser to Ike
30 Fact-check
31 "You betcha!"
33 Hysteria curber
34 Late philanthropist Joan
35 Widespread reaction
36 Fellow forgets to shave before kissing girlfriend; ref cites him for …
42 Some bow ties
43 Compliment to the chef
44 "If only ___ listened!"
45 Acquisitions person
47 Right away
49 Looks over
53 The Great White North
54 Popular brand of stationery
56 Dance floor remains empty at debutante party; ref rules it a …
57 Tennis call
58 Join hands?
59 Smooth
60 Big inits. in movies
61 Freestyle jumps
64 Handsome marriageable man enters room; ref signals …
66 A neighbor
68 One end of the spectrum
69 Multitude
70 Duke of 63-Down
71 Farm call
72 Gorgeous lady enters room; ref signals …
75 Tito Puente's specialty
76 Reading site
80 Name used in indignant questions
81 Lincoln or Ford
82 Secured, as carpet tacks
84 Suffix with dual
85 Revenue sources
86 At a loss
87 Guy gets grabby on first date; ref penalizes him for …
94 Suffix with period
95 Naval base?
96 Rock's Mötley ___
97 Salon options
98 Wallace who wrote "Ben-Hur"
99 Unseen character in a Beckett play
100 First name in gossip
102 1930's have-nots
106 Lovers embrace passionately in public place; ref declares …
110 Unmeaningful
111 It's often found in a bar
112 Railroad chartered in 1832
113 Balladeer's aid
114 Iditarod race destination
115 Radiant
116 Russet-colored liquors
117 Release
118 Icky stuff

DOWN

1 Ruined
2 Score of zero
3 Theater company that thinks big
4 Guy acquires girl's phone number but waits too long to use it; ref signals …
5 Eat late
6 It precedes a cast party
7 Weigh
8 "Mississippi ___" (Denzel Washington film)
9 Shade provider
10 Contract negotiator: Abbr.
11 Come unglued
12 Body part repaired by tympanoplasty
13 Folk singer McKenna
14 Remain
15 9-Down material
16 Leftover
17 "A merry heart ___ good like a medicine": Proverbs
21 Normandy campaign objective
24 Strong support
25 Thrash
27 Surrounds with trees, say
32 Focus on
35 Edit for TV, maybe
36 Potentially insulting
37 Writer Ephron
38 Bright time
39 Birmingham-to-Montgomery dir.
40 Tom Clancy hero
41 Typical Rick Moranis film role
46 Overhauled

Jul/Aug

monday
27   208

tuesday
☽ ## 28   209

wednesday
29   210

thursday
30   211

friday
31   212

saturday
1   213

sunday
2   214

s	m	t	w	t	f	s
						1
2	3	4	5	6	7	8
9	10	11	12	13	14	15
16	17	18	19	20	21	22
23	24	25	26	27	28	29
30	31					

AUGUST

32. GRIDIRON GLOSSARY

BY PATRICK MERRELL / EDITED BY WILL SHORTZ / 11-07-04

ACROSS

1 How one must win in volleyball
6 Like most bicycle tires
11 World Service provider
14 King of comedy
18 Element #5
19 Stradivari's teacher
20 Breeder's interest
22 What one gets from the hot dog vendor when paying with a $5 bill?
24 Who we are
25 Mesabi Range wealth
26 Under cover?
27 A stone may have one
28 Not allow
30 Platinum blonde cheerleaders?
34 Basic learning, for short
35 Tom, Dick and Harry
36 It's murky
37 Singer Baker or Bryant
39 Carpet type
41 Horror maven Craven
42 Clears
46 Home viewers' HDTV's?
51 Where the Danube ends
53 Words before ghost or doctor
54 Some fancy footwork
55 Manage, with "out"
57 Of lesser size
58 Star followers
60 Ill-treats
62 One who flies south in the winter
63 Most popular beer brands at the concession stands?
69 Easily bribed
70 Bids one club, e.g.
71 Marineland performer
72 Time for a spring roll?
74 1990 Broadway one-man play
75 33-Down output
78 Lodge sign
82 Led
84 Trash talk?
87 Babysitters' charges
88 Sinker's call
90 Eye part
91 Molokai colonist, once
92 Tufted tweeter
95 E and G, e.g., in D.C.
97 "Halloween ___" (1983 flick)
98 Rule barring players from dating cheerleaders?
104 Stuart monarch
105 Mo who unsuccessfully ran for president in 1976
106 Some pats
107 Flout the Volstead Act
109 Associated with
111 Untackled players?
115 Mukluk attachments
116 "And if that weren't bad enough …"
117 Sea inlet: Var.
118 Many ages
119 Part of E.S.T. : Abbr.
120 Payments made before a deal is completed
121 Politico Kefauver

DOWN

1 Jul. 4 happening
2 2-Down reader, right now
3 Track event?
4 Cause of wrinkles
5 Aware of
6 Large decks
7 Spectral image
8 Bleated
9 "…, ___"
10 Hägar creator Browne
11 Store restriction
12 Neighbor
13 N.Y.S.E. listings
14 Subject of much praise
15 Été reading
16 Lend ___
17 Fits snugly
20 Overseas whistle blower
21 Longtime record label
23 Start of Massachusetts' motto
26 Hosp. workers' org.
28 Picks at random
29 With 86-Down, 2002 British Open winner
31 1997 Aaliyah hit "The One ___ My Heart To"
32 Impulse
33 Name on many a children's book
35 Laugh syllable
38 Ones on a bench together
39 One in 100: Abbr.
40 Sot's sound
42 Connected two computers, say
43 Permanently
44 Cuts carbs, maybe
45 1986 #1 Starship hit
47 What a sphere lacks
48 Home of Al-Azhar University
49 Chair filler
50 Arctic gull
52 Work done to scale
56 One with a pole position?
59 More fit
60 Rx prescribers

August

61 Russian export, familiarly
63 Cool
64 Loose, as stones
65 Choose
66 Roman imperator
67 Sufficient, informally
68 Beforehand: Abbr.
69 Third piece
73 Gum
75 Head warmer?
76 Suffix with oct-
77 Troop grp.
79 Fresh from the oven
80 ___ ten (long odds)
81 Unsettling
83 Child's puzzle
85 Detonator
86 See 29-Down
89 Refined
92 Jousting contests
93 Snacks packaged in trays
94 One evidently not filing
   a flight plan
95 Monkey Trial defendant, 1925
96 Having four parts: Prefix
98 Prize money
99 Gland: Prefix
100 Where a do is done
101 Certain side dishes
102 Chicago-based critic
103 Hopeless
104 Auspices
108 Bio
110 Geezers' interjections
111 Old "Up, up and away"
    sloganeer
112 Dearie
113 Thrice uno
114 60's campus grp.

CIVIC HOLIDAY (CANADA, MOST PROVINCES)
BANK HOLIDAY (SCOTLAND)

monday

3 215

tuesday

4 216

wednesday

5 217

thursday

○ 6 218

friday

7 219

saturday

8 220

sunday

9 221

s	m	t	w	t	f	s
						1
2	3	4	5	6	7	8
9	10	11	12	13	14	15
16	17	18	19	20	21	22
23	24	25	26	27	28	29
30	31					

AUGUST

33. NO MORE ACHES

115 Bubkes
116 "As if!"

DOWN

1 1930's Brazilian import
2 "For want of ___ …"
3 1-Down, e.g.
4 Do, say
5 Soviet Physics Nobelist ___ Tamm
6 Stout sites
7 City named for an Indian chief
8 Dies ___
9 Shed
10 Nest builder
11 Heir, usually: Abbr.
12 Inane
13 Walkers on hot coals
14 1930's-60's power couple
15 God attended by two ravens
16 The Panthers of the Big East
17 Some beans
19 Akin to
20 "O.K."
24 Muskogee tribe
26 Bawl out in no uncertain terms
30 Spelling of Hollywood
31 Claude who starred in TV's "Lobo"
32 Malarial episodes
33 White wine apéritifs
34 First mate
35 Undergrad degs.
36 Decoration from Eliz. II
37 Atoll with no electric lights?
38 French companion
39 Fashionable dress
40 Year the emperor Frederick II died
41 Start fresh
42 Skiing documentaries?
44 Hoover rival
45 Artist from Barcelona
47 Hole puncher
49 Vast amount
51 N.L. or A.L. team
52 They ripple on bodybuilders
54 Small fry
55 Apt. units
57 Talk a blue streak?
58 Legal thing
59 Name meaning "she-bear"
60 Hallmark card text, often
63 "___ pasa?"

BY CON PEDERSON / EDITED BY WILL SHORTZ / 11-14-04

ACROSS

1 Woeful
4 Checks the growth of
8 Japanese porcelain
13 Turkeys
18 One that's similar
20 Pressed
21 Studio feed
22 Major nickel exporter
23 Large place where elks gather?
25 Where squabbling neighbors live?
27 Positions
28 Off the wind
29 Driving aid
30 Starchy fixin's
32 Kipling pack leader
35 Spread managers
37 Large amount of money
40 Partner, with "the"
43 Mason's request?
45 Hendrix of 60's music
46 Public rap
48 For ___ an emergency
49 Prefix with linguistics
50 Large bills, informally
51 Red Cross course, for short
53 1970's fad participant
56 Clark's companion
57 Encouraging words
61 Muscat native
62 Defunct pro sports org.
63 Genetically improved grain?
65 Typesetters' needs: Abbr.
67 "___ pray"
69 Impertinent types
70 In a stack
72 Merriest
75 Actress Thurman
76 Copy illegally
77 Milk: Prefix
78 Everyday
82 Dryly said
83 Town on the Humboldt River
84 Complaint that one didn't get enough presents?
88 ___ lab
89 Couple abroad
90 Edwards, for one
91 Adjutants
92 Marcher's woe
93 Wing
94 Primatologist's study
98 Housed, as a student
101 Cattle prod?
106 Clock's slowing down?
109 Directly
110 Tea biscuit
111 Overturns
112 Personal interview
113 Not easygoing
114 Chutney fruit

August

monday
10 222

tuesday
11 223

wednesday
12 224

thursday
☾ 13 225

friday
14 226

saturday
15 227

sunday
16 228

s	m	t	w	t	f	s
						1
2	3	4	5	6	7	8
9	10	11	12	13	14	15
16	17	18	19	20	21	22
23	24	25	26	27	28	29
30	31					

AUGUST

34. "NATIONAL" HOLIDAY

BY KUMAR BALANI / EDITED BY WILL SHORTZ / 11-28-04

ACROSS

1 Causes of bickering
6 "Rock'd the full-foliaged ___": Tennyson
10 Solar event
15 See 24-Down
19 Prayer recipient, maybe
20 Binge
21 1962 tennis Grand Slam winner
22 Sudden clouding-over, maybe
23 Step 1 of a Thanksgiving dinner
27 Thatcher's place
28 One of the angels on "Charlie's Angels"
29 Mount
30 Undersides of overhangs
34 Interpret
35 Cared for lovingly
38 Elevate
39 Extended time
40 Young hog
41 Step 2
47 Walks
48 Send off
49 Game equipment
50 Work of Homer
52 Cooling treats
53 Look-alike
54 Opponent of Stalin
55 Work of Juvenal
57 The "one" in the phrase "draw one"
58 Ray who founded McDonald's
59 Actress Flockhart
60 Step 3
66 Blue Diamond canful
67 "Phooey!"
68 Tirade
69 Elements of a biblical miracle
70 Cooling treat
71 Sawbuck halves
72 Beach sandal problem
76 Spill producer
77 Santa ___
78 Creepy crawler
79 Having the toilet paper roll put on the "wrong" way, e.g.
80 Step 4
85 Responds to gravity
86 "Dies ___"
87 Loosens
88 Make retroactive
92 "Laugh-In" segment
93 Plate
94 Register
95 Procrastinator's promise
96 Show windedness
97 Step 5
106 "___ Rock"
107 Matrimony
108 Perfidious
109 Hello or goodbye
110 Polar expedition, e.g.
111 Competed in a rodeo event
112 Genesis maker
113 Like some jackets

DOWN

1 Line in geometry
2 U.N. agcy. dealing with jobs
3 Sore throat producer
4 Blacken
5 Western heroes
6 Spirit of a people
7 Be idle
8 Time to get back to work: Abbr.
9 Police action
10 Not static
11 Macaulay's "___ of Ancient Rome"
12 Actress Gardner
13 Officiate, briefly
14 Big real estate firm
15 Vagabonds
16 Desert V.I.P.'s
17 Poetry
18 Over
24 With 15-Across, need, slangily
25 Small goose
26 Certain sorority member
30 ___ bar
31 Sight-related
32 Hole in one, assuredly
33 Small wind instruments
34 Fasten again
35 1970's sitcom title character
36 Dynamite
37 British rule in India
39 Approve of
40 Card
42 Stair posts
43 Putdown of those with whom one disagrees
44 ___ point
45 Imitative
46 Spanish point
51 Burn
53 Oversees
54 Much-heard
55 Composer Saint-___
56 Gobs
57 Ruin
58 Winter celebration
59 Nickel and dime
60 High

monday
17 <small>229</small>

tuesday
18 <small>230</small>

wednesday
19 <small>231</small>

thursday
● 20 <small>232</small>

friday
21 <small>233</small>

saturday
22 <small>234</small>

sunday
23 <small>235</small>

s	m	t	w	t	f	s
						1
2	3	4	5	6	7	8
9	10	11	12	13	14	15
16	17	18	19	20	21	22
23	24	25	26	27	28	29
30	31					

The New York Times

BY ELIZABETH C. GORSKI / EDITED BY WILL SHORTZ / 12-05-04

ACROSS

1 Family-friendly ratings
4 Natl. Grapefruit Mo.
7 "How Dry ___"
10 Fragrant hair ointment
16 They may go for big bucks
18 Fat substitute
20 Ones fit for kings and queens?
22 Attractions at the Thanksgiving parade in old Pennsylvania?
24 Disturbs
25 Volcanic rock
26 Holder of an insect's DNA?
28 Big Ten rival: Abbr.
29 Not waver from
32 Chantilly's department
33 Go after
35 Not likely to pose nude
36 Recipe amts.
38 Many a vacationer's need
44 Fab Four film
45 Fraternity letter
46 "Don't bother!"
48 Longtime Dolphins coach
49 Syndicated advice column from a couch potato?
53 Kind of garage
55 Mattress filler
56 Kooky Kovacs
57 Leaves after a meal?
58 Complain
59 Weight
61 Dublin hangouts
63 Opinion piece
64 Reverse image?
68 Deduce
72 Dress material for a ball
74 Make-up person?
75 "The Lion in Winter" star, 1968
76 What the Lincoln Memorial faces
79 Poets' feet
83 Two years before Claudius was murdered
84 Undo a secession
85 Office manager's oversight of felt-tip pens?
89 Captain's order
90 Adam's first wife, in Jewish folklore
91 Article in France-Soir
92 Captain of 1960's TV
95 Handles
97 ___ the Great (boy detective)
98 Parlor transaction
99 Fundamental physics particle
100 Disney or Whitman
102 Pitcher
104 "Oz" network
105 Background of roses, irises, etc.?
112 Woody vines
114 Stew morsel
115 Ones using "the facilities"?
118 Cordial
119 Season, in a way
120 "Now, about ..."
121 Does greenhouse work
122 Suffix with expert
123 Actor Vigoda
124 Carrier to Oslo

DOWN

1 Composer of "Oedipus Tex" and "A Little Nightmare Music"
2 Opaque watercolor technique
3 The "surf" in some surf 'n' turf dinners
4 Strength
5 Seasonal worker
6 Ann Patchett novel "___ Canto"
7 Author Calvino
8 So SoHo
9 Neither fem. nor neut.
10 Prepares, as a surface for painting
11 Prefix with -pod
12 "Serpico" author
13 Violist's clef
14 Judge
15 Latin 101 verb
17 Cousin of reggae
19 Pushover
20 Arrondissement resident
21 Bruisable things
23 Berlin-born Sommer
27 Drawing site
30 Italian noble family name
31 Exodus figure
34 Neurology, oncology, cardiology, etc.
36 Round stopper, for short
37 Fries or slaw
39 Archipelago unit: Abbr.
40 "I'm serious!"
41 Bazooka part
42 Portoferraio is its chief town
43 You can catch them on a beach
45 Raison d'___
46 Building support
47 Linda in 1990's news
50 Singer Tucker
51 ___-American relations
52 French fire

monday
24   236

tuesday
25   237

wednesday
26   238

thursday
☽ 27   239

friday
28   240

saturday
29   241

sunday
30   242

s	m	t	w	t	f	s
						1
2	3	4	5	6	7	8
9	10	11	12	13	14	15
16	17	18	19	20	21	22
23	24	25	26	27	28	29
30	31					

The New York Times

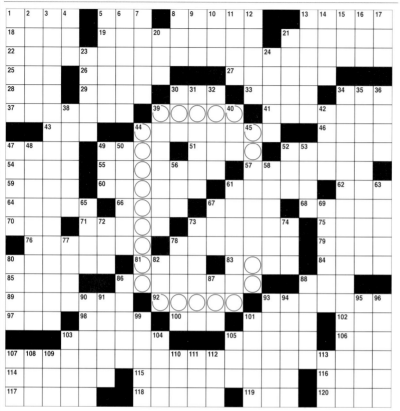

102 Rum ___ Tugger ("Cats" cat)
103 It may be hard to keep
105 Newspapers
106 Road map no.
107 Calvin Coolidge lived up to his reputation as a man of few words when he …
114 Sweden's largest lake
115 George W. Bush, as a managing general partner of baseball's Texas Rangers, traded away …
116 Without ___ (unprotected)
117 The only U.S. president whose vice president ran against him to succeed him was John …
118 Get rid of
119 Ace reliever Robb
120 Understands

DOWN

1 More lascivious
2 Slothful
3 Presidents 117-Across and 44-Down both died the same day in 1826 …
4 "Ixnay"
5 Tickled
6 Coffee orders
7 Bad lighting?
8 Suffix with odd
9 Anguilla is part of it: Abbr.
10 Writer Fleming
11 Takes a jog
12 Pot creators
13 1976 uprising site
14 Stepped (on)
15 Anthem contraction
16 Young fellow
17 QB Manning
20 Cover, in commercial names
21 Cat sound?
23 Have a spot ___
24 Rock's Van ___
30 Object
31 Roofer, at times
32 Works at
34 John Quincy Adams, as U.S. secretary of state, was the man who actually drafted …
35 Ronald Reagan is the only U.S. president who was also president of a …
36 The Kennedys, e.g.
38 Nevertheless
39 Peace interrupter
40 Rocks, so to speak
42 See 56-Down
44 A U.S. president who was also an architect, musician and inventor was …
45 Yanqui

By ELIZABETH C. GORSKI / EDITED BY WILL SHORTZ / 12-12-04

ACROSS

1 Sharp-billed diver
5 Home of Russell Cave Natl. Monument
8 Mediterranean resort island
13 Made off with
18 Sicilian mount
19 Frank Delano Roosevelt's phrase "New Deal" came from a book by …
21 Like the north wind
22 Theodore Roosevelt, who was never known as the modest type, is the only U.S. president ever to give an inaugural address …
25 Homer Simpson outburst
26 Camera lens setting
27 Ocean floor
28 Fort Smith-to-Little Rock dir.
29 Target MTV viewer
30 Horned viper
33 One-armed bandit

34 Educational cable network
37 Puts through again, as paper in a copier
39 "When ___ hear from you?"
41 Extremely significant
43 Eggs
44 Kingston resident, e.g.
46 Self-titled WB sitcom
47 Together, musically
49 One-named singer/actress
51 Abound
52 1994 Peace Nobelist Peres
54 Go bad
55 Some fund-raisers
57 Global divide
59 911 responders, for short
60 Below-the-belt
61 Really beats
62 Sorority letters
64 Hate
66 Architect of Spain's Miró museum
67 Early sixth-century year

68 "Stormy Weather" singer
70 It's due in Venice
71 Love
73 Like weightlifters
75 Enter
76 States positively
78 Baroque piece
79 Revolutionary Trotsky
80 1997 Demi Moore title role
81 Circus reactions
83 Work ___ many levels (succeed)
84 Tracy's mom, in "Hairspray"
85 Needle case
86 Dirty Harry, e.g.
88 Maven
89 Bears, on Wall Street
92 Country singer Black
93 Some Diego Rivera works
97 Tax
98 Glove
100 Ushered
101 One going to the dogs?

BANK HOLIDAY (UK EXCEPT SCOTLAND)

monday

31 243

tuesday

1 244

wednesday

2 245

thursday

3 246

friday

4 247

saturday

5 248

sunday

6 249

s	m	t	w	t	f	s
		1	2	3	4	5
6	7	8	9	10	11	12
13	14	15	16	17	18	19
20	21	22	23	24	25	26
27	28	29	30			

SEPTEMBER

The New York Times

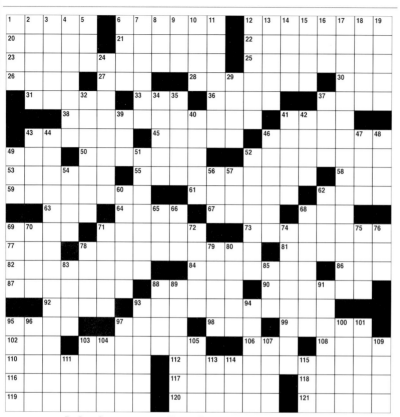

BY LEE GLICKSTEIN AND NANCY SALOMON / EDITED BY WILL SHORTZ / 12-19-04

103 Befuddled
106 Land's end?
108 Kind of theater
110 "Darned if I know"
112 Result of a vacuum cleaner mishap?
116 One tooting a horn
117 Joins in
118 Busted
119 Diving areas
120 Hate with a passion
121 Primary strategy

DOWN

1 Blows away
2 Ding Dong alternatives
3 "The Compleat Angler" author Walton
4 Strong Greek wine
5 Nutritionist's fig.
6 Goes belly up
7 Raymond of "Dr. Kildare"
8 Chats online, for short
9 Course list abbr.
10 Baltic port
11 Cool brews
12 "You don't even want to know the alternative!"
13 Canada's Point ___ National Park
14 Polish
15 Wedding fling?
16 Bird: Prefix
17 Cost of a mail-order bride?
18 Building material
19 Clipped
24 Get bug-eyed over
29 Gorgons
32 Cold weather protector
34 Took care of
35 Tread stealthily
37 Alfred E. Neuman feature
39 7' 5" Ming
40 Made fancy
41 Little digit
42 Lake tribe
43 Mrs. Copperfield
44 Order to a power plant worker?
46 Small types
47 Cheney's predecessor
48 Hoity-toity one
49 Prince of Broadway
51 Kite aid
52 Nourished the mind
54 Early Nebraskans
56 Bro
57 Jackie's second
60 Coarse

ACROSS

1 Fan's sound
6 One of the Brothers Karamazov
12 Collapsible lid
20 Ran very slowly
21 Like most sonnets
22 Multiply like an amoeba
23 Amazed telegram recipient's cry?
25 One who gets a reaction
26 In order
27 Jerk
28 Letter getter
30 "Dennis the Menace" airer on old TV
31 One going down fast
33 PC key
36 Palliate
37 Indian butter
38 Midshipmen's gridiron gains?
41 Fairylike being of myth
43 Where a lot of fed. govt. workers live
45 Playwright Peter who wrote "Marat/Sade"
46 TV Guide data
49 Water, chemically
50 Ignored, as authority
52 Calling "chicken," perhaps
53 Colorful circle
55 Saw out of the blue?
58 Supporting
59 Got milk
61 Correspondence
62 Famous murder defendant of the 1920's
63 Silent authority?
64 Unstimulating
67 Lengthy sentence
68 Carol contraction
69 Silent army
71 Some multiplayer deals
73 "You don't say!"
77 Book before Esther: Abbr.
78 What a local news broadcast leads with?
81 Announce
82 Darkening
84 Impetuously, perhaps
86 Gloomy guy
87 "Don't worry"
88 Clinton's first secretary of defense
90 Relatively rare
92 Falls behind, in a way
93 Tramp class?
95 One of 12 popes
97 "See ya"
98 Namath put it on the map: Abbr.
99 Grounds for a good night's sleep?
102 Table scrap

September

LABOR DAY (US, CANADA)

monday
7 250

tuesday
8 251

wednesday
9 252

thursday
10 253

friday
11 254

saturday
☽ **12** 255

sunday
13 256

s	m	t	w	t	f	s
		1	2	3	4	5
6	7	8	9	10	11	12
13	14	15	16	17	18	19
20	21	22	23	24	25	26
27	28	29	30			

SEPTEMBER

BY FRANCES HANSEN (1919–2004) / EDITED BY WILL SHORTZ / 12-26-04

ACROSS

1 Subordinate ruler
7 Former rulers of Egypt
14 Came out of sleep, old-style
20 Put on the same level
21 Treeless plain
22 It may be in a torpedo
23 Start of a verse
26 Fringe, maybe
27 "Ici on ___ français"
28 Hon
29 Take-home
30 Was bright
32 Code cracker's comment
34 Sentimental song
38 Slight manifestation
39 Maligned
44 ___ Cologne (skunk of old cartoons)
45 Climb
46 Cast off
47 Fa followers
48 Verse, part 2
54 Hoary
55 Zero population
56 Small goose
57 Spray displayers
58 Word of possibility
59 Token taker
60 One way off a ship
61 Vestibule
62 Itsy-bitsy biter
63 Record notation
64 Paradigm of happiness
66 "___ figlia dell'amore" (Verdi quartet)
69 Walks heavily
70 Festive
71 Timberjack's tool
74 Broadcasting
75 "Dred" novelist
76 Life-or-death situation
77 Manufacturing center?
78 Verse, part 3
82 Livy's "Lo!"
83 Henri's high
84 Diamond complement
85 Counseling, e.g.
86 Ice alternative: Var.
88 Scooby Doo's co-creator
90 In the habit of
92 Big mouth, slangily
93 "The Syncopated Clock" composer Anderson
94 Had something
95 Lots
99 Sicilia, e.g.
101 Bern, Geneva and Zurich
106 End of the verse
111 Kindle
112 Resembling a chanterelle mushroom in flavor
113 Mimosa family member
114 Right from the factory
115 Soul
116 Some speech sounds

DOWN

1 Shakers, e.g.
2 Cool shade
3 Mild reproofs
4 Loser's cry
5 She sprang from Zeus's head
6 Skinless
7 Grp. associated with dens
8 Record store section
9 Correct ending
10 Big game fish
11 Recent delivery
12 Sound asleep?
13 Kind of monitor
14 Hard-rock center
15 Classified
16 Gucci of fashion
17 The Green Hornet's valet
18 Discharge
19 Runs out of steam
24 W. Coast setting
25 Sweetie pie
30 Base coach's urging
31 Not say directly
33 Pilgrimage to Mecca
34 Abraham's ___ (heaven)
35 Miss Quested of "A Passage to India"
36 Jitterbug variety
37 Court call
38 Capital of East Flanders
39 Get lost in a brown study
40 Wachovia or Chase Manhattan, briefly
41 Ocean liner?
42 Big name in bonding
43 Chain component, perhaps
45 Hotfoot it
46 1953 film title hero
49 Catch
50 "Show Boat" heroine
51 "Much ___!"
52 Colliery carriers
53 Covering everything
60 Move like a puma
62 Suspended porch piece
63 Pull
64 Giant
65 Inter ___
66 Pitney's partner
67 Tennyson's Arden
68 Medieval charging need
69 Pub potable
70 Davis of Hollywood
71 Longed
72 Ready to be played, in a way

September

73 Herbert Marx, familiarly

73 Herbert Marx, familiarly
75 "Tosca" villain
76 Roman encyclopedist
79 Cassowary's cousin
80 Latin word on a monument
81 Subject of
   "The Motorcycle Diaries"
87 Go around
88 Ancient serfs
89 Like farmland
90 West Jordan resident
91 "Epistulae morales" writer
93 Big name in computer software
94 Take steps
95 Diego Velázquez's
   "Lady With ___"
96 Take on
97 Ample, poetically
98 Together, in music
100 End of a New Year's classic
102 Start of a Christmas classic
103 Ocean danger
104 Catch but good
105 Places to get steamed
107 Slick
108 A as in Austria
109 Org. that registers boxers
110 Something to drive off of

monday

14 257

tuesday

15 258

wednesday

16 259

thursday

17 260

ROSH HASHANAH (BEGINS AT SUNSET)

friday

● **18** 261

saturday

19 262

s	m	t	w	t	f	s
		1	2	3	4	5
6	7	8	9	10	11	12
13	14	15	16	17	18	19
20	21	22	23	24	25	26
27	28	29	30			

SEPTEMBER

sunday

20 263

39. WHAT PEOPLE MIGHT SAY BEFORE DOING THIS PUZZLE

BY PATRICK MERRELL / EDITED BY WILL SHORTZ / 01-09-05

ACROSS

1 Garlicky seafood dish
7 Vacuum tube
13 Trig function
19 What imbibers might feel
20 Desk-clearer
21 Great Plains tribe
23 The optimist …
26 Bill extras
27 Tower supports
28 John
29 Contingency plans address them
30 Collector's suffix
32 High spots
33 Brain section
34 The pessimist …
43 Overly studious types
44 Fielders' choices
45 It precedes one
46 Alphabet trio
47 The Green Wave, in college sports
50 Famed caravel
52 Cousin of Wm. and Robt.
55 The self-hypnotist …
60 Approved
61 Site of the Grimaldis' 700-year reign
62 Pull (in)
63 It's seen in the dark
66 "McHale's Navy" craft
69 Good looks
70 Super-duper
71 Sharply reprimand
73 Rap music's Kris Kross and others
75 The conformist …
83 The sun
84 Some cheeses
85 Yellow
86 U.N. workers' grp.
87 Kind of sch.
88 Israeli port
90 Fife accompanier
92 The therapist …
99 Function
100 Docs prescribe them
101 Tour de France challenge
102 Señores say it in unison
103 Stuffed Indian dish
106 "Hey! … yeah, you!"
109 New Rochelle college
113 The mentalist …
117 Author of "Guerrilla Warfare"
118 Cry on a baseball field
119 Money left at a secret location, maybe
120 Duel item
121 Rural hangouts
122 Bean and others

DOWN

1 Presumptuous one
2 Popular fragrance from France
3 On ___ with
4 Race around the earth?
5 Mathematical constants
6 How baby girls are often dressed
7 When said three times, a W.W. II film
8 One having second thoughts
9 Followers: Suffix
10 Sash
11 Rubber bones, e.g.
12 Urge
13 With 72-Down, a signature on the Declaration of Independence
14 Pennsylvania's northwesternmost county
15 "Out of the question"
16 Kwik-E-Mart clerk on "The Simpsons"
17 Land
18 It began in 1908 with 34 agts.
22 Caucasus native
24 Impose ___ on (outlaw)
25 "Oh, pooh!"
31 Risked
32 Cause of a big blowup
33 China's ___ Yutang
34 Cross inscription
35 One side in an annual football game
36 Leavings
37 Arabian Sea borderer
38 Wound, but not fatally
39 Up and ___
40 Where the 2004 Rep. Natl. Convention was held
41 Untrue
42 Successful kick
48 Four-stringer
49 Topper
50 Constrained, with "up"
51 Form 1040 declarations, for short
52 "Holy mackerel!"
53 Lad clipped by Floyd the barber
54 Prim and proper, e.g.: Abbr.
56 Like most lips
57 Show feelings
58 Overseas broadcaster, in brief
59 Clear the tape
63 Gaping holes
64 Number below cinco on un teléfono

September

INTERNATIONAL DAY OF PEACE

monday

21 264

AUTUMNAL EQUINOX 21:18 UTC

tuesday

22 265

wednesday

23 266

thursday

24 267

friday

25 268

saturday

☽ 26 269

s	m	t	w	t	f	s
		1	2	3	4	5
6	7	8	9	10	11	12
13	14	15	16	17	18	19
20	21	22	23	24	25	26
27	28	29	30			

YOM KIPPUR (BEGINS AT SUNSET)

sunday

27 270

110 Not cornered?
112 Good cheer
115 Declaration from a die-hard beer drinker?
118 Bright annual
120 Tutor of 12-Down
121 Artless one
122 Dispatch boats
123 Class of "1984"
124 Campus life
125 Moon goddess

DOWN
1 Tennis edge
2 Suffix with puzzle
3 Where many songs are heard
4 Procrastinator's shopping day, maybe
5 Harmless
6 Hoover Dam's style
7 Wearer of a famous ring
8 Place to sleep, slangily
9 Spock, e.g.: Abbr.
10 Not switched off
11 Spanish card suit
12 Hated ruler of old
13 N.J. summer setting
14 Conference need
15 Pillager
16 Thurston Howell type
17 Fan mail recipient
18 Part of binary code
19 Once, once
25 Rush
28 Pink tip
32 White House worker
34 Androphobe's aversion
35 Bric-a-___
36 Permanently, after "for"
37 White house?
38 1970's White House inits.
39 Unwavering
40 Trap
42 Jewish scholar Berlin and others
43 Largest college fraternity in the U.S., in brief
44 Bridge support
45 "I'd hate to break up ___"
51 Assay need
53 Tries desperately to get
54 Pursue closely
55 Landlord's paperwork
56 New Haven's nickname
59 Guru's hangout
60 Word with mess or press
63 Some beachgoers
64 Cry when the lights come on

BY BRENDAN EMMETT QUIGLEY / EDITED BY WILL SHORTZ / 01-16-05

ACROSS
1 Elementary biology subject
7 Compaq product
14 Judicial inquest
20 Six Flags Elitch Gardens city
21 Coming from the factory, say
22 Look around
23 Aim
24 Typical, as a beer?
26 Last degree
27 Output of un philosophe
29 General in Chinese restaurants
30 Matter of interpretation
31 Psyched up
33 Oxford offering, for short
35 Sainted historian
36 Beer-drinking singer of the 1970's?

41 Record label for Whitney Houston and Usher
46 Melodramatic outburst
47 Turkish Empire founder
48 Messenger ___
49 Ones who've been tapped on the shoulder
50 Valued advice-giver
52 Purpose
53 Inferior, as beer?
57 Samoan staple
58 Mr. Potato Head piece
60 Penetrating
61 Superlatively slippery
62 Part of A.S.A.P.
64 Eat like ___
66 They'll show you the neighborhood
68 Cry by one who's disgusted by beer?
71 Pertaining to stars
73 Become vexed

74 "The Spirit" cartoonist Will
78 College offering
79 Bow-wielding boy
81 D-Day vessel
82 Prefix with meter
83 Expert in beer?
85 Class-conscious grp.?
87 Football stat
89 Rat tail?
90 Mate
91 Needed a bath
93 Princess from Alderaan
94 Greets nonverbally
97 Having the experience of years of beer drinking?
100 Assignment
102 Narrow inlet
103 1961 John Updike story set in a grocery store
104 Popular surfing site
108 Dust jacket feature

Sep/Oct

65 Like some consonants
67 Gibberish
69 Prefix with byte
70 Sound that means "Back off!"
71 Defunct treaty acronym
72 Michael Jackson's 1987 boast
75 Letdown after awaiting a reply
76 Comedian Izzard
77 Buddy of 1940's baseball
78 Go across
80 Card table action
81 Best Supporting Actor winner
   for "Ed Wood"
84 Lend, informally
85 Exhibitor of Jumbo the elephant
86 Kind of cross
88 "Put ___ on it!"
91 Madras Mr.
92 December celebrations
95 Each
96 Stein title subject
98 Like a ravine
99 Escarole alternative
101 Close relative
104 Velvet ant
105 New World abbr.
106 "The answer ___!"
107 Big name in compilation albums
108 Judge's seat
109 Actress Swenson
111 Pointed arch variety
113 Skilled stalker
114 Unaffectedness
116 Córdoba kinswoman
117 Follower of Benedict
119 Zippo

monday
28 271

tuesday
29 272

wednesday
30 273

thursday
1 274

friday
2 275

saturday
3 276

sunday
◯ 4 277

s	m	t	w	t	f	s
				1	2	3
4	5	6	7	8	9	10
11	12	13	14	15	16	17
18	19	20	21	22	23	24
25	26	27	28	29	30	31

OCTOBER

41. PLEDGE OF ALLEGIANCE

BY DAMON J. GULCZYNSKI / EDITED BY WILL SHORTZ / 01-23-05

ACROSS

1 Accomplices
8 Andean treasure
11 Suffix with sermon
14 Slightest trace
19 Wardrobe
20 Popular fish sandwich
22 "Christmas bombing" target
23 Klutzy dog's habit?
25 Matter of debate
26 Farm call
27 Bathroom on wheels?
29 ___-Pei (dog)
33 TV palomino
35 Homer Simpson's next-door neighbor
36 Paid the penalty
37 One holding corn bread?
40 Run in syndication, maybe
43 O'Neill and others
44 Like many shorelines
45 Where to see a mummy: Abbr.
47 Prince Valiant's wife
50 Include
51 Next in line for slavery?
58 Did a third draft of
60 Credit for driving people home?: Abbr.
61 What surprises can come out of
62 Wrapping weights
64 Crew equipment
66 Cantina cooker
67 Famous rallying cry ... and a hint to eight other answers in this puzzle
75 Starship princess
76 Do a number
77 East Indian heartwood
78 It keeps the ball rolling
82 "Apocalypse Now" setting
83 Doles out differently
88 Get a workout via horseback riding?
92 Spinnaker site
93 Flashback, e.g.
94 "___ will not!"
95 Baker's gadget
96 Actress Busch
99 Sibling of un frère
102 Renowned razor sharpener?
105 Multitudes
108 Instructors' org.
110 Live nomadically
111 Multitude
112 Visit to Ben & Jerry's?
116 Live
117 Recurring Nintendo character
118 Annoy people by blowing a fan on them?
125 Cutting parts
126 Perk up
127 Veteran, on Veteran's Day
128 Mower maker
129 Weightlifter's unit
130 It's made in Japan
131 Make more attractive

DOWN

1 Rude dude
2 Legend on the ice
3 Plan for patients, for short
4 Alley-___
5 It may be in stitches
6 Neat, as a beard
7 Málaga missus
8 Polo Grounds standout
9 Duisburg's locale
10 Hit-and-run situation?
11 Tryster with Tristan
12 Pueblo dweller
13 Irving Bacheller's "___ Holden"
14 Trick-taking game
15 Can't help but
16 Bananas
17 Hit, in basketball
18 "Jingle Bells" sleighing locales
21 More fit
24 Suffix with theater
28 Round Table knight
29 Caveman's tool
30 Multitude
31 Nicad's cadmium component
32 Fixed up
34 Patrick's "Ghost" co-star
38 Melville's "___ Cereno"
39 Automaton-themed play of 1921
41 "This is so-o-o relaxing!"
42 "Why should ___ you?"
46 Sideshow attraction
48 Café alternative
49 Shady plot
51 Savior
52 Idyllic settings
53 Book between Amos and Jonah: Abbr.
54 NASA weather satellite
55 Teatro ___ Scala
56 Put to sleep
57 Faithful, to a Scot
59 Besmear
63 Divider of Paris
65 Tieup
67 Touched down
68 Nightly monologue deliverer
69 Property lawyer's concern

October

monday

5 278

tuesday

6 279

wednesday

7 280

thursday

8 281

friday

9 282

saturday

10 283

s	m	t	w	t	f	s
				1	2	3
4	5	6	7	8	9	10
11	12	13	14	15	16	17
18	19	20	21	22	23	24
25	26	27	28	29	30	31

sunday

☽ **11** 284

The New York Times

BY JOE DIPIETRO / EDITED BY WILL SHORTZ / 01-30-05

ACROSS

1 Place to buy ice cream
8 Family subdivisions
14 Go after
20 Taking a break
21 The one that got away?
22 1959 #1 hit for the Fleetwoods
23 Stick-in-the-mud types
24 Rich man's wife, often
26 Jacks and such
27 Whirlpools
29 Schubert's Symphony ___ Minor ("Unfinished Symphony")
30 Yahoo competitor
31 LAX listing: Abbr.
32 Common locales for film brawls
34 Bel ___ cheese
36 A new start?
37 Consequence of war
39 Kind of bean
40 Stone memorial
42 "What have I done?!"
43 Flutter
46 Italian car, briefly
48 Mil. fliers
52 See 69-Across
53 Word on a shoppe sign
57 Tab
58 Usually low-paying work
60 Amazon menaces
61 Impassive
63 Copy, in a way
64 Fictional captain
66 Duchamp contemporary
67 Like some windows
69 With 52-Across, former "Saturday Night Live" cast member
72 Out there
74 "Go on"
75 Boobs
78 "Happy Anniversary" writers
81 Egypt's Mubarak
82 Langston Hughes poem
84 Opulence
88 Barfly's binge
89 Versailles votes
90 Creation of 1948
91 The Fleetwoods, for example
92 Pond youngsters
93 Gotten slower with age
96 Contracted group
98 Cap ___ in the Baseball Hall of Fame
101 Snack
102 Chop alternatives
108 Pull
109 Pens, possibly
111 Most rough, at sea
112 Nasser's org.
113 Kind of particle

114 "Shallow ___" (2001 Jack Black movie)
115 Most withdrawn
116 "Finnegans Wake" wife
117 Illinois
121 Work unit without much work
124 Classic Darrell Hammond impersonation
125 Office buildings often have them
126 French inn
127 Prefix with day or year
128 Not prompt for
129 Psychedelic, in a way

DOWN

1 Zero on the screen
2 Completely
3 English policy makers
4 Some sneakers
5 Favorite activity, slangily
6 Columbus, in N.Y.C.
7 Turn over
8 Live Aid founder Bob
9 Famed New York eatery
10 Certain posers
11 Popular ice cream
12 Antique auto
13 Speak to the owner?
14 Words of agreement
15 Trendy New York area
16 USA competitor
17 Ones with degrees
18 Foul-mouth
19 Enamored of
25 Rest on top of
28 "And how!"
32 Mama's boy
33 In an entangled state
34 Like some crosses
35 Luxury Toyota
38 Critic with big sideburns
39 Feudal estate
41 Get from ___ (progress slightly)
44 City served by McGhee Tyson Airport
45 Opposing force
46 Forbear
47 Ripped
49 Smooth jazz feature
50 Visage on a fiver
51 Part of a road
54 Stuff in baskets
55 Be afraid to
56 Lively wits
59 Eggs
62 Fortune profilee, for short
65 "That's gotta hurt!"

October

COLUMBUS DAY
THANKSGIVING DAY (CANADA)

monday
12 285

tuesday
13 286

wednesday
14 287

thursday
15 288

friday
16 289

saturday
17 290

sunday
18 291

s	m	t	w	t	f	s
				1	2	3
4	5	6	7	8	9	10
11	12	13	14	15	16	17
18	19	20	21	22	23	24
25	26	27	28	29	30	31

OCTOBER

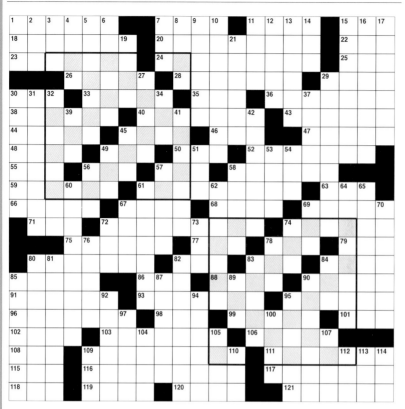

BY DERRICK NIEDERMAN / EDITED BY WILL SHORTZ / 02-06-05

ACROSS

1 Panhandle site
7 In ___ rush
11 Two-wheeler
15 Farm mother
18 Defendants' protests
20 Health resorts
22 Call ___ day
23 Chaim Weizmann, for one
24 Orbit
25 Shook hands, say
26 Capital of Jamaica [black]
28 Beloved British figure [black]
29 District of Colombia?
30 Platoon V.I.P.
33 Noted Twain portrayer [black]
35 N.Y.C. subway
36 Chloe's love, in myth
38 Military pilots
40 Fortress
43 April, May and June, to Daisy Duck
44 Misdirect, maybe
45 Suffix with 44-Across
46 Long time
47 Yellowish shade
48 When schoolkids go to bed early [black]
49 Actress Ullmann
50 U.K.'s locale
52 Common hospital name
55 Baseball Hall-of-Famer Roush
56 Grown-up kit
57 Writer/humorist Joe [white]
58 Basic belief
59 Eying [white]
61 The sixth of Henry VIII
63 Big inits. in bowling
66 Rotten
67 Solitary
68 Easy two-pointer
69 ___-Turkish War
71 Hwy.
72 Abandoned child
74 Postwinter flood
75 Author Gordimer
77 Famed bluesman [black]
78 Cry on "The Simpsons"
79 Dog in "Dondi" [black]
80 Hobo
82 Newspaper adv. unit
83 Criticize
84 Bankrolls
85 Russian emperor in 1800
86 Tokyo, formerly
88 Bidding site
90 Send
91 Freed
93 Way of thinking
95 100 centimos
96 Begin to flourish
98 Excellent service
99 Ship's mooring aid [black]
101 Med. land
102 Actress Lillian
103 Some fuel-carrying ships
106 Old ___, Conn. [black]
108 Actress Sue ___ Langdon
109 Colonial craft [white]
111 Rotten
115 ___ culpa
116 What black and white squares do on a chessboard
117 Leather factory
118 Round no., maybe
119 Predicament
120 Husky vehicle
121 Stowe character

DOWN

1 Relative of a chisel
2 Circular greeting
3 Year abroad
4 Kind of feeling
5 Given name among old Chinese leaders
6 Old Dodgers manager called "Smokey"
7 Enzyme suffix
8 Spring festival honoree
9 Geritol target
10 Unruliness
11 One of the three B's
12 Annoyed
13 John of radio's "Information, Please!"
14 Tuck in
15 Follower of samedi
16 Studios
17 "The Piano Lesson" painter
19 Small runway craft, for short
21 Walk shakily
27 First World Series color broadcaster, 1955
29 Result of black's move from the upper-left board to the lower-right board
30 Proved pleasing
31 Emergency safeguard
32 Yelled
34 Beginner
37 Devout
39 R & B singer Brian
41 Picked up the check
42 Some corporal punishment
45 Early morning hour
49 Chance

October

monday
19
292

tuesday
20
293

wednesday
21
294

thursday
22
295

friday
23
296

UNITED NATIONS DAY

saturday
24
297

SUMMER TIME ENDS (UK)

sunday
25
298

s	m	t	w	t	f	s
				1	2	3
4	5	6	7	8	9	10
11	12	13	14	15	16	17
18	19	20	21	22	23	24
25	26	27	28	29	30	31

OCTOBER

44. WHAT A PICTURE IS WORTH

The New York Times

BY JOEL KAPLOW / EDITED BY WILL SHORTZ / 2-13-05

ACROSS

1 Reserve
8 Sending a duplicate, for short
13 Hold up on the road
19 $5,000
20 Something to file away
21 Best Supporting Actor winner for "Cocoon"
22 Easily snapped
23 Social reformer Bloomer
24 Aleve alternative
25 10¢
27 ___ diagram
28 Often-unpaid worker
29 City on the Danube
30 What you will
32 Vodka brand, briefly
34 Make like
35 Prose piece
38 Diplomat Boutros Boutros-___
40 Giants manager before Durocher
41 Dropout's goal, perhaps: Abbr.
42 100 kopecks
45 ___ Rafael
46 Group of dyes
47 More than a little
48 $100
51 Great leveler
52 Dog star?
54 Dawn deity
55 Seek damages
56 Indiana Jones's topper
58 Kilns
62 Only O.K.
64 Does nothing
66 25¢ or $1
69 Problem for a deejay
70 Secure overhead, say
71 School V.I.P.
72 It may be played
73 $1
76 Problems addressed by podiatrists
77 Utah resort
78 Site of the Pont de Normandie
79 Paris, for one
81 Understand
83 Cry in cartoons
84 A conductor might pick it up
87 It may be labeled sl. or obs.
88 What 15 answers in this puzzle appear on
90 Military flier's acronym
93 Part of some uniforms
94 Terrarium youngster
95 Better-chosen
96 "I'll take that as ___"
97 Something to do at 77-Across

98 Words following a superlative
100 Big test
104 Debut of 6/1/1980
105 Color
108 Human body's hardest substance
111 Poetic preposition
112 Continue
114 Rime
116 $1
119 Constitutional
120 Uses as a target
122 Tennessee county named for a jurist who co-founded Memphis
123 See 91-Down
124 Bar lineup
125 1¢ or $5
126 Anthony who won a Grammy for "What Kind of Fool Am I?"
127 Sizing up
128 Chants

DOWN

1 Stain
2 "Good Christian Men, Rejoice" and others
3 "Hands down" and "cold feet"
4 These may be picked
5 90° from norte
6 Puzzle out
7 Oldtime daggers
8 U.R.L. ender
9 $1,000
10 Frequent Cleese co-star
11 Ruhr refusals
12 $50
13 $10
14 "Consider the job done"
15 Joan who sang "I Love Rock 'n Roll"
16 Lot statistic
17 Cricket, at times
18 50¢
20 Al ___ (guerrilla group)
26 Sporter of three stars: Abbr.
31 They often differ
33 Percolate slowly
36 Prince Valiant's son
37 Stooges' laughs
39 Tagging along
43 Skylike
44 Wasn't straight with
46 Bully, often
47 Medical breakthrough of 1998

Oct/Nov

monday
☽ 26 299

tuesday
27 300

wednesday
28 301

thursday
29 302

friday
30 303

HALLOWEEN *saturday*
31 304

DAYLIGHT SAVING TIME ENDS *sunday*
1 305

s	m	t	w	t	f	s
1	2	3	4	5	6	7
8	9	10	11	12	13	14
15	16	17	18	19	20	21
22	23	24	25	26	27	28
29	30					

NOVEMBER

The New York Times

BY DANIEL C. BRYANT / EDITED BY WILL SHORTZ / 02-20-05

ACROSS

1 "That's ___"
6 Clear the tables
9 They stand by doors
14 See 120-Down
18 Untrustworthy one
19 Word to a team
20 Glory
21 Outback runners
22 Checking the help wanted ads?
25 Duke of ___, Shakespearean character
26 Surround
27 Curse
28 Personal histories
30 Have a change ___
32 Oldest technological univ. in America
33 County across the bay from San Francisco
34 Scrabble piece in a retirement home?
38 Speech enlivener
42 Quint's name
43 ___ Pieces
45 Archaeologists, by profession
46 Pudding ingredient
47 Where to find teachers and students
50 School grp.
52 Spooks
53 Send
55 Protected, in a way
56 ___ Garcia (Indian Ocean atoll)
58 Actress Sommer
59 One meter x one meter x one meter
61 Still
64 Catch up to again
66 Birthplace of the Roman poet Sextus Propertius
68 "Roots" Emmy winner
70 Certain believers
74 Defiant cry
76 Free
78 Former Crayola color
79 Trading grp.
82 Some hooks
84 Sent duplicates to, briefly
86 ___'acte
87 Certain outbreak
89 Title acronym of 1980's TV
90 Hay fever sufferer, e.g.
93 Indian title
94 They can make a strong person weep
96 Summer complaint
98 "Wine-dark" sea
100 Ajar

102 Complaint precipitating the American Revolution?
105 Poor prognosis
106 MSN competitor
107 Vatican masterpiece
108 Relating to a mystic Jewish sect
111 Like some robes
113 First name in linguistics
117 Caspian tributary
118 For turning a screw when you lack a screwdriver, there's … what?
121 Peevishness
122 "Good ___!"
123 Top-notch
124 He said "A lie told often enough becomes truth"
125 Bloomingdale's rival
126 Displaying no emotion
127 Stage
128 Miffed

DOWN

1 "___ of Wine, a Loaf of Bread …"
2 Certain bond, slangily
3 German/Polish border river
4 Force into
5 Mysterious gift
6 Clientele
7 Mil. branch
8 Spanish wines
9 Breakwaters
10 It can be a lot
11 Year in Edward the Confessor's reign
12 Cape wearer
13 Guided
14 Where pa took his boy for a whipping?
15 Mine, to Mimi
16 1973 Gore Vidal political novel
17 Interrogates
19 Nerve
23 Lightens
24 City due west of the Everglades Parkway
29 Certain silicates
31 It's done in France all the time
33 How football's Jerry was addressed as a boy?
34 Site of the Potemkin mutiny
35 Part of an auto safety inspection
36 Plains orphans
37 Worked on the Street

November

39 Trompe l'___
40 Long haul
41 To be at the Colosseum
44 Prefix with center
48 Italian question starter
49 "I only have eyes for you," e.g.?
51 With 57-Down, ancient
54 Lothario?
56 Spanish lady
57 See 51-Down
60 Erie-to-Phila. dir.
62 Rosinantes
63 Former map inits.
65 W.W. I army: Abbr.
67 "___ had it!"
69 Yadda yadda yadda
71 Judo teacher
72 Woman's shoe
73 Pilgrim's destination
75 Hockey's Tikkanen
77 "___ who?"
79 Expectant cry
80 ___ colada
81 "___ falls on him who goes
to seek it": Cervantes
83 Young newt
85 Marksman
88 Hair net
90 Winner, for sure
91 Outside the law
92 Grp. of battalions
95 Helps out quickly?
97 Severely criticize
99 More vast
101 Take
103 Checking a box, say
104 "The Sonnets of Orpheus" poet
108 Centers
109 Solo
110 Virologist Jonas
111 Weight-loss drug combo fen-___
112 Wild plum
114 Farm cry
115 Jeanne to Jean, peut-être
116 Fix
119 Mañuel's uncle
120 With 14-Across, a famous "cave man"

s	m	t	w	t	f	s
1	2	3	4	5	6	7
8	9	10	11	12	13	14
15	16	17	18	19	20	21
22	23	24	25	26	27	28
29	30					

monday

2 306

tuesday

3 307

wednesday

4 308

thursday

5 309

friday

6 310

saturday

7 311

sunday

8 312

The New York Times

BY ELIZBETH C. GORSKI / EDITED BY WILL SHORTZ / 02-27-05

ACROSS

1 Where to see a Constable or Turner, with "the"
5 Personal papers
12 Sales off. folders
17 Former N.S.C. chief Scowcroft
19 Columnist Huffington
20 Treelike cactus
22 Combination of 64- and 74-Across
24 Kate ___, vocalist for rock's B-52's
25 English composer of "Dido and Aeneas"
26 1960's Cubs pitcher Paul
27 Accuracy
28 Dustin's "Midnight Cowboy" role
29 Actress Zellweger
30 Strands, during winter
31 Swelled
33 Rajahs' wives
35 Swipes
38 Anat., for one
41 Papal name
42 Carriers
43 Bandleader Xavier
44 Dash gauge
46 Tiny creature
48 Ad ___
49 Mrs. in Chicago history
50 "Whoever you ___ love you" (Hal David lyric)
51 Command to a dog
52 "Romanian Rhapsodies" composer
54 Score clock no.
55 See 70-Down
57 "Law & Order" role: Abbr.
59 Queue after Q
60 Suffix with Canton
61 Literary inits.
64 Ticker symbols?
67 Engine part
68 Former Russian orbiter
71 Has
73 Assam appellation
74 See 22-Across
79 Maestro ___ de Waart
80 Get comfortable
83 See 103-Across
87 Yard sale caveat
88 City of Light sight
90 Cousin of Fido
91 ___ Fountain
92 Ranch visitor
93 Reservations
94 Branch of the Dakota Indians
96 Actress Turner
98 Bit of butter
99 First name in courtroom fiction
100 Chopin's "Raindrop" and "Butterfly," e.g.
101 Claim
103 83-Across works
105 Exams for future docs
107 Red River city
110 Seven Sisters units
112 Walkway
113 "Take that!"
115 It's touching
116 22-Across and 70-Down
118 Folks angling for a job?
119 "Oh yeah, that'll happen!"
120 April 1 baby
121 Antiknock agent
122 Forward-thinking type
123 Horrific

DOWN

1 Cook's meas.
2 Polish-born pianist Rubinstein
3 Land in ancient Rome
4 Passes
5 Author Roald
6 Supper table scrap
7 Went through carefully, as clues
8 Clip joint
9 Before birth
10 Wrap
11 Fan's belt
12 Writer James and others
13 Squiggle
14 Venue for this puzzle's theme
15 Jog
16 MGM Studios owner
18 Occupies
20 Livens (up)
21 West Wing group
23 They're sung in joyful hymns
27 More apt to bite
29 Visit again
32 Andy of old comics
34 Light on Broadway
36 Louvre locale
37 "Funny Girl" composer Jule
38 New York's ___ Island
39 Cause a highway holdup?
40 Miss Congeniality she's not
42 "Look on the bright side …"
43 Seventh heaven
45 Park activity
47 Cause for an appointment with a cardiologist
49 Numerical prefix
53 Erstwhile bloc letters

November

monday
☾ **9** 313

tuesday
10 314

VETERANS DAY   *wednesday*
REMEMBRANCE DAY (CANADA)
11 315

thursday
12 316

friday
13 317

saturday
14 318

s	m	t	w	t	f	s
1	2	3	4	5	6	7
8	9	10	11	12	13	14
15	16	17	18	19	20	21
22	23	24	25	26	27	28
29	30					

sunday
15 319

The New York Times

108 "Ferris Bueller's Day Off" actress
109 Stumble
110 7 and 11
111 Pros

DOWN

1 Unfreeze
2 Slangy rejection
3 Reading unit?
4 March time
5 Crag
6 See print
7 Exclamation an angel loves to hear
8 Trite
9 Do not disturb
10 Three-time Burmese prime minister
11 Alway
12 Pride, e.g.
13 They're each worth two F.G.'s
14 "Scenes of Clerical Life" writer, 1857
15 It's full of brains
16 Moves briskly
19 Martial arts star featured in "Romeo Must Die"
20 ___ king
21 Cuts to specific dimensions?
23 Savings option, briefly
27 Goals
29 Adult insect
30 Photographer Goldin and others
31 Like octuplets?
32 "Cool!"
33 Place of rest
34 Vultures were sacred to him
38 Singer Nicks
39 Bit of reality?
40 Sister of 34-Down
41 It has one stripe on its back
42 Ask the director of church singing?
43 Cross with
44 Smallville family
46 Place for a catnap?
47 Joe Hardy's temptress
48 Over
51 Put film into
52 Imparts
54 "Punkin" coverer
55 Covers with coal dust
57 Boorish

By Mike Torch / Edited by Will Shortz / 03-06-05

ACROSS

1 Former New York Philharmonic conductor Mitropoulis
8 Most down
14 Potential lifesaver, for short
17 Struck
18 Advanced Latin class reading
19 Con tender?
22 Works off and on as a hospital resident?
24 Weather Channel topic
25 Lotful
26 Syrian, say
27 Not for free
28 Watch
29 Breathe during an ice storm?
35 "Take ___ a sign"
36 Spring time in Paris
37 Close call
39 They're not normal
44 Scoundrels
45 Pioneering electrical engineer
49 Scuba gear gaskets
50 Pharmaceutical ointments
52 Wound
53 "Thong Song" rapper
54 Jai alai arena
55 Rossini opera setting
56 Tricked twin
57 Come up with
58 New family member, maybe
59 Raids at the Colossus?
63 Traditional Sunday fare
66 Hallmark of a perfect game
67 Seine sights
71 College with the mascot Lord Jeff
72 Threatens to topple
74 Web mag
75 Big name in satellite radio
76 Entertainer
77 Unspecified alternative
78 Cold-cocks
79 "___ bragh!"
80 Air producer
82 Eight-day observance
84 Classical opener
85 Signal receiver
88 Eat for fun?
92 It has moles: Abbr.
95 Like many company publications
97 Straight
98 Course list?
99 1970's-80's House speaker
100 Executive of an apple juice company?
106 Worrywart's words
107 Gruesome

November

monday
16 320

tuesday
17 321

wednesday
18 322

thursday
19 323

friday
20 324

saturday
21 325

sunday
22 326

s	m	t	w	t	f	s
1	2	3	4	5	6	7
8	9	10	11	12	13	14
15	16	17	18	19	20	21
22	23	24	25	26	27	28
29	30					

By John Greenman / Edited by Will Shortz / 03-13-05

ACROSS

1 Dom DeLuise comedy
6 Field protector
10 Performer with a balancing act
14 Lord's worker
18 The Capris' "There's ___ Out Tonight"
19 Playwright Capek
20 Exile isle
21 Ally of the Missouri, once
22 Lulu of a predicament?
24 Good season for kite-flying?
26 Alchemist's life prolonger
27 Shark's place
29 Listing
30 Halfhearted
32 City near Le Havre
33 Supermodel Bündchen
35 Treat like dirt
37 Sorry souls
39 Have something at home
40 Penn Station inits.
41 Dog that's up on the latest fashions?
44 ___ Spiegel (German magazine)
47 Beach on the Costa del Sol
49 Yes, in Yokohama
50 Meaningful little cough
51 Welfare payments, e.g.
52 W-2 ID
53 Greeting from a dwarf?
58 Meanies' miens
60 "China Beach" star Dana
62 Kingklip catchers
64 Film score composer Morricone
65 It rises when you get a raise
67 Nada
68 Pleasantly sweet
70 Boutros-Ghali's successor
71 Nuanced
74 Price fixer
75 Ocean liners?
77 Browbeating sleepyhead?
79 Not working
82 Celebrity biographer Hawes
83 Stereotypical lab assistant
85 In the manner of
86 Florida's ___ National Forest
88 Cross-referencing word
89 Lower abdomens?
94 Near Eastern port
95 Brought forth
96 Unfamiliar
97 Small wood
99 Went up
101 Mr. Miniver, in "Mrs. Miniver"
102 Lasting aftereffects
104 Makarova of tennis
105 Resolved
108 Goes down
111 Thick foam on beer?
113 Apple-polishers' perches?
116 Camembert alternative
117 About
118 Revolutionary War patriot Putnam
119 The blahs
120 Practice, pugilistically
121 Alternative to 50-Across
122 Memo abbr.
123 Make gender-neutral

DOWN

1 It's temporarily in
2 Valentine for Valéry
3 Extent of damage
4 Prison punishment
5 Features of some cameos
6 XXX part
7 Symbols of safe passage
8 Tightened, in a way
9 Complete in every respect
10 Attach, as a patch
11 Ivy League team
12 Deny oneself
13 Bucko
14 Tone down
15 Sell online
16 "Good Times" matron portrayer
17 With 54-Down, a derby, e.g.
19 Diva ___ Te Kanawa
23 Lab tube
25 Late name in Mideast politics
28 1910's heavyweight champ Willard
31 Not bright
34 Gossipy squibs
35 Is laid up
36 Slivovitz or kirsch?
38 Pascal or newton
39 It can knock people out
40 45 alternatives
42 French wines
43 Trough site
44 Wagonfuls of feathers?
45 Mrs. Jock Ewing
46 Cover anew, as a plot
48 Oblique
51 Beneficiary
54 See 17-Down
55 Movie with the Oscar-nominated song "Papa, Can You Hear Me?"

November

monday
23 327

tuesday
☽ 24 328

wednesday
25 329

THANKSGIVING DAY *thursday*
26 330

friday
27 331

saturday
28 332

sunday
29 333

s	m	t	w	t	f	s
1	2	3	4	5	6	7
8	9	10	11	12	13	14
15	16	17	18	19	20	21
22	23	24	25	26	27	28
29	30					

49. LABORATORY MAZE

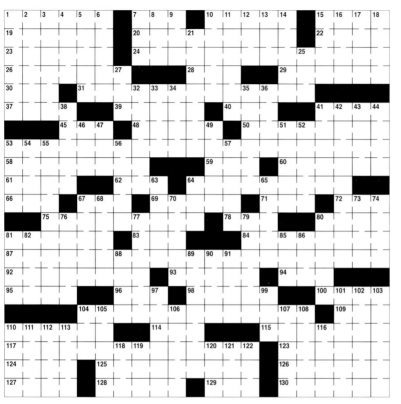

BY PATRICK MERRELL / EDITED BY WILL SHORTZ / 03-20-05

When this puzzle is completed, solve the maze in the grid, traveling through the openings in the squares, beginning at 69-Across, ending at 103-Down … and passing over the word spelled at 71-Across 18 times. As you proceed, the consecutive letters of 71-Across will always be in their correct order, in straight lines reading forward, backward, up or down.

ACROSS

1 Speaking sites
7 D.C. lobbying grp.
10 Olympian Griffith Joyner, familiarly
15 One covering the infield
19 Elocuted
20 Like most magazine personality tests
22 Melville work
23 Passé
24 Smell victory, in a lab maze?
26 Attempted activity in "The Barber of Seville"
28 Suffix with ideal
29 Eye lasciviously
30 Org. with a key-holding eagle in its logo
31 Cheat, in a lab maze?
37 See to
39 Computer woe
40 "The Confessions of ___ Turner"
41 Rights grp.
45 Double curve
48 "Miss ___ Thompson," 1953 musical film
50 Part of a food pyramid
53 Hit a dead end mazewise?
58 Term
59 Set
60 Mark and Shania
61 Asia's ___ Sea
62 Assent in les Alpes
64 Feather holder
66 Thither
67 Jazz guitarist Montgomery
69 Begin
71 Lab maze runner
72 Pit sight
75 Works around town?
78 ___ milk
80 Stuffed food
81 Materialize
83 Article of the Constitution about the judiciary
84 Dove
87 Get weary solving a lab maze?
92 Salute site
93 Done in
94 Make, in arithmetic
95 Recipe info: Abbr.
96 Sch. where Samuel Morse was a professor of art
98 End of MGM's motto
100 Mag. sales info
104 Does some lab maze-solving?
109 Book after Ezr.
110 Head post
114 Epitome of simplicity
115 Go over again
117 Solve a lab maze almost inaudibly?
123 Brave cover
124 "My Fair Lady" is based on his work
125 Foundations
126 Cars known for backfiring?
127 Options for traders
128 High lands
129 "Tasty!"
130 Clue for a car mechanic

DOWN

1 Maze participant
2 Veiled threat
3 Austronesian language
4 'Vette option
5 Make a new excavation
6 Gland prefix
7 Bounced check letters
8 Olds mobile
9 Accompanier of thumbs and ears
10 Frat rushees, often
11 Pros with cons
12 Plains Indian
13 Actress Aniston, familiarly
14 Scott who wrote "Island of the Blue Dolphins"
15 Soap made by Dial
16 Marc Antony's love
17 Parks in Alabama
18 "Every man will be a ___ if he can": Thoreau
21 Arrives suddenly without formality
25 Pommes frites seasoning
27 State biggie
32 One of a Hindu trinity
33 Q.E.D. part
34 Designer Gernreich
35 Had passed its expiration date
36 Outermost of the Aleutians
38 Transfer
41 Play the role of
42 Garbo film "Queen ___"
43 Trim
44 Deliverer of many pkgs.
46 Didn't play
47 ___ generis (unique)
49 Anticipatory
51 Stars, in Kansas' motto
52 Stop from getting dry
53 Mate's hello
54 International coin
55 Convey
56 One taking a gander?
57 Different cuts
63 "Let me repeat …"

monday

30 334

tuesday

1 335

wednesday

○ 2 336

thursday

3 337

friday

4 338

saturday

5 339

sunday

6 340

s	m	t	w	t	f	s
		1	2	3	4	5
6	7	8	9	10	11	12
13	14	15	16	17	18	19
20	21	22	23	24	25	26
27	28	29	30	31		

DECEMBER

50. TWO, PLEASE

The New York Times

BY PATRICK BERRY / EDITED BY WILL SHORTZ / 03-27-05

ACROSS

1 Tunnel of love vehicle
5 St. Crispin's Day mo.
8 Antarctic explorer Sir Vivian
13 Scarlett's heartthrob
19 In hopeless shape
21 Pasty
22 George who directed "Creepshow," 1982
23 Home of the Houdini Museum
24 Drawing ___ (two, please)
26 Lost ___ (two, please)
28 Hooked letter
29 "The Premature Burial" author
30 The "I" of I. M. Pei
31 Hard ___ (two, please)
35 From ___ on (two, please)
41 Pipe residue
42 [This is heavy!]
43 City on the Mohawk
44 Area north of Leicester Square
46 San Antonio-to-Ft. Worth dir.
47 European capital whose name is Greek for "wisdom"
50 Bygone women's magazine
53 Omar of "The Mod Squad," 1999
55 "Cyrano de Bergerac" author
57 ___ on (two, please)
60 Highly reactive metal
61 As well
62 Simón Bolívar's birthplace
65 Cycle starter
66 Cotton press output
69 Appian Way traveler
71 Speak at length
72 Stimulate
73 Ring from Hawaii
74 Wedding hiree
76 Send over the edge
78 Besides
80 White ___ (two, please)
85 Extreme
87 Frigg's husband
88 Refuse
89 Get one's second wind
90 Return filler, maybe: Abbr.
92 "Secret Window" star, 2004
95 Tree houses
96 Prima donna problem
97 Münster Mister
99 ___ it out (two, please)
102 Religious ___ (two, please)
106 Sewed up

107 Comedian Philips
108 Frightened sound
109 Roller ___ (two, please)
116 ___ capsule (two, please)
120 Be too hasty about
121 Assurance to a jokester
122 They may be irresistible
123 Set right
124 Generic, as products
125 Western coalition?
126 Steppingstone to pres., maybe
127 Torch bearer?

DOWN

1 Australian wild
2 A while ago
3 Mystique
4 Ruler of yore
5 Pick up
6 Back from the dead, maybe
7 Strings you might pull
8 Popular game in Old West saloons
9 "Forgive ___ trespasses …"
10 Barrio hooligans
11 Sew up?
12 Have in the interim
13 Tennyson's "Enoch ___"
14 Blubber
15 67-Down offering: Abbr.
16 Acceptance sans proof
17 "My Wicked, Wicked Ways" author Flynn
18 Tyrolean cry
20 Certain soldier
25 More elegant
27 Order to disperse
32 Taken
33 Beds (down), in Britain
34 Hometown ties
35 Drones
36 Cut, as glass
37 "Little Caesar" character
38 Game similar to euchre
39 Architect Alvar ___
40 Forehead wiper's exclamation
45 Grp. that includes Nigeria
48 Condition
49 Come clean about
51 Test subjects
52 High-hat type
54 Popular brandy flavor
56 National anthem adopted in 1980
58 Planetarium roof
59 It's never left at sea

December

monday

7 341

tuesday

8 342

wednesday

☾ 9 343

thursday

10 344

HANUKKAH (BEGINS AT SUNSET)   *friday*

11 345

saturday

12 346

s	m	t	w	t	f	s
		1	2	3	4	5
6	7	8	9	10	11	12
13	14	15	16	17	18	19
20	21	22	23	24	25	26
27	28	29	30	31		

sunday

13 347

DECEMBER

The New York Times

109 General Motors repair shop slogan?
114 Old telecom giant
115 Sonneteer's sundown
116 Glorify
117 Not exaggerated
118 Horse or dog lead-in
119 Drill wielder: Abbr.
120 "The Silence of the Lambs" director
121 Pieces of nine?
122 It may be smoked

DOWN

1 Goodyear alternative
2 Have no accomplices
3 Perfect prairies?
4 Match
5 Salutation starter
6 Having one sharp, musically
7 Verbum ___ (word of God)
8 No challenge
9 Swedish actress Hasso
10 Stars and Bars org.
11 Ballot abbr.
12 Investment house T. ___ Price
13 Cajole
14 Airline convenience
15 "No need to elaborate"
16 Far from flustered
17 Pitchman?
20 Piglet
25 Blow up
26 Cash cache
28 Windshield feature
32 Second hand
33 Bull Moose's party: Abbr.
34 They're no longer hitched
35 TV receiver
38 Sounds of contentment
40 HBO alternative
41 Bunker Hill general
44 Pad sharer
45 Bruce who played Watson
48 Mother ___
49 Short of
50 Rake over the coals
51 Result of playing around with a knife on a patio?
52 Land ___ (bargain-hunt successfully)
53 Yankee skipper
55 Go back
58 Ballot rosters
59 Waldorf salad ingredient
60 Gymnastics coach Karolyi and others

BY CON PEDERSON / EDITED BY WILL SHORTZ / 04-03-05

ACROSS

1 Fairy queen
4 Nike rival
10 She turned Odysseus' men to swine
15 Suffix with 65-Down
18 Bump off
19 It recounts the Fall
21 Condescending one
22 Storm producer, once
23 Price abbr.
24 Irate restaurant force?
27 Milliner
29 In due course
30 Turns on
31 J. R.'s mother
32 Was attractive (to)
36 "In & Out" star, 1997
37 Kind of shark
38 Travel medium
39 Hotel awning?
42 Quick approval: Abbr.

43 Festoon
46 Did a double take?
47 Original Luddite ___ Ludd
48 TV series about proper departure etiquette?
50 Jazz variety
54 Firm boss: Abbr.
56 S-curve
57 Old Portuguese currency
59 Less inept
61 Lafayette's forces
63 Part of B.C.E.
66 Procrastinator's mantra
67 "Shalom"
68 French naval post?
70 Petal product
71 Carries on steadily
72 Topic of many a lie
73 "___ My Heart ..."
74 Oar pin
75 Two-seated carriage

77 Mile or mil
78 Some are corny
79 Ovidian infinitive
80 Dreaming à la Ravi Shankar?
86 Time meas.
89 Come to rest
90 Établissement éducatif
91 Sneak ___
92 Like an estate that a father wills to his children?
97 With 112-Down, exemplar of madness
98 Cartoon company
99 Hill once seen on the Hill
100 More than miffed
103 Zero for Nero
104 Neck parts
107 Old fool
108 Sodium ___ (cleansing agent)

December

monday

14 348

tuesday

15 349

wednesday

16 350

thursday

17 351

friday

18 352

saturday

19 353

s	m	t	w	t	f	s
		1	2	3	4	5
6	7	8	9	10	11	12
13	14	15	16	17	18	19
20	21	22	23	24	25	26
27	28	29	30	31		

sunday

20 354

The New York Times

BY NANCY NICHOLSON JOLINE / EDITED BY WILL SHORTZ / 04-10-05

ACROSS

1 Breaks
10 Places for notes
14 All's partner
19 Not a long shot, by a long shot
20 Rap sheet word
22 ___ Jackson, a k a Ice Cube
23 "If I had a little humility, I'd be perfect"
24 "I am the literary equivalent of a Big Mac and fries"
26 It's heard in the Highlands
27 Beethoven work in E flat
29 Accord
30 "___ Pagliaccio"
34 New Jersey's ___ Bay
36 Sounds at the Simpsons'
37 Million-selling Harry Connick Jr. album
40 All done
43 Habituate
44 "I have never been hurt by anything I didn't say"
47 Zodiac symbol
53 Own
54 "___ Gold"
55 Barbershop girl
56 Stops
57 Squeal
58 Ibsen's Gabler
62 Louisiana locale
63 Fellini film, with "La"
66 Henri, e.g.
68 "I guess it just proves that in America anyone can be president"
70 "Swan Lake" role
72 Drug
73 "I am a deeply superficial person"
77 Ida. neighbor
78 Pub servings
83 Trowel wielder
84 Wetlands sights
86 Classic opener
88 Latin singer Anthony
89 Deighton's "The ___ File"
91 Praise
93 Fan
94 "The English Patient" setting
95 "I am beautiful, famous and gorgeous"
99 Womanizer
101 Capers
102 Letters for the dear departed
103 "The Purple Cow" rhyme scheme
107 Points the finger at
109 Name in fragrances
111 Cornmeal mush
113 Filament

116 Ordnance component
120 "Everything you see I owe to spaghetti"
122 "I respect a man who knows how to spell a word more than one way"
126 One of the Coen brothers
127 Video game name
128 Weave
129 Film classic of 1953
130 "What ___?"
131 Witches in "Macbeth," e.g.

DOWN

1 Louis XVI lost his
2 Maintain
3 1917 shoe debut
4 Stage direction
5 Laura Bush's alma mater, for short
6 Pro
7 Room offerer
8 Certain necklines
9 Lake ___, lowest point in Australia
10 Italian staple
11 No longer the same
12 Post-New Year's activity
13 Dope
14 Stubborn person's word
15 Appealed
16 Thick-skinned one
17 New York City avenue
18 Gurus
21 Cut
25 Group of 112-Down
28 Working stiff
31 "___ ain't broke ..."
32 Clamor
33 Run up
35 Calendar abbr.
37 A lot
38 "I've ___!"
39 Playwright Rice
41 Gilbert and Sullivan title heroine
42 Like some confrontations
45 Border guard's request
46 Suffix with book
48 Comparatively embarrassed
49 Staff symbol
50 City whose name seems to consist of two opposites
51 ___'acte
52 Scan
55 High rating
59 Painter Schiele
60 Trust in
61 Expel

December

WINTER SOLSTICE 17:47 UTC   *monday*

21 355

tuesday

22 356

wednesday

23 357

thursday

☽ **24** 358

CHRISTMAS   *friday*

25 359

KWANZAA BEGINS   *saturday*
BOXING DAY (CANADA, UK)

26 360

sunday

27 361

s	m	t	w	t	f	s
		1	2	3	4	5
6	7	8	9	10	11	12
13	14	15	16	17	18	19
20	21	22	23	24	25	26
27	28	29	30	31		

DECEMBER

53. SCIENTIFIC AMERICAN

BY ELIZABETH C. GORSKI / EDITED BY WILL SHORTZ / 04-17-05

ACROSS

1 Realtor, e.g.: Abbr.
4 Things that can be rolled over, for short
8 Delicateness
12 Foes of Lenin
20 Science fiction writer Frederik
22 Not taking sides: Abbr.
23 Lab gel
24 Deli order
25 Gazetteer datum
26 Fill until full
27 Corn syrup brand
28 Helping
29 Place with a board
30 Where 67-Down taught
32 Make lace
33 Away, in a way
34 Beat up on
35 E.R. lifelines
36 "Excuse me ..."
37 Go by foot, slangily
39 Greek war goddess
40 Sound quality
42 Ward (off)
44 Attacked
49 One who's taken in
51 Flight suit stitching
53 First name in motorcycle jumping
54 Dangerous strain
55 Reason for a bounced check: Abbr.
56 Scientist's question
57 Santiago charger
58 Bird's home: Var.
59 Bohr who was a contemporary of 67-Down
60 Locations for some schools
62 ___ 'acte
63 Stay in the sun too long
64 "Au contraire!"
65 ___ Laredo, Mexico, on the Rio Grande
67 True or false: Abbr.
68 Spiritual path
70 Old Big Apple paper, with "the"
72 Big D.C. lobby
74 "I've Got the World on a String" composer
75 Belle-___-en-Mer, France
76 Discount rack shorthand
77 Work on the edge?
78 Cable inits.
79 "That ___ lie!"
80 Extension
82 Famed statement by 67-Down
84 Proofreader's notation
85 Darlin'
86 Industrial container
87 Days of ___
88 Colorado native
89 "E.R." regulars
90 First strategy
92 Big record label
93 Contrite type
94 "There but for the grace of God ___"

DOWN

1 Like the Navajo language
2 Bouts
3 Proposal by 67-Down
4 Notwithstanding
5 Mirrors may show them
6 Psychologist's study
7 W.W. II gun
8 "Courage!"
9 Type size
10 Rebounds
11 Suffix with Jumbo
12 Observation, part 3
13 How bitter enemies attack
14 High-end viola
15 Louis, for one
16 Where a Laker may live
17 Indian honorifics
18 Northumberland river
19 Nintendo rival

95 Part: Abbr.
96 Come of age?
97 Prestigious schools
99 Literary inits.
101 Squabble
103 Early astronaut
105 Soul
106 Gradually withdraw
107 Unit of storage
108 "Frasier" role
109 Bailout key
112 Small sheds
113 Mayo's locale
114 Company that has its ups and downs
115 Small snowfall
117 Jerome Kern tune "___ Forget"
118 Woody Allen's feeling, often
120 Empress of the Blues ___ Smith
122 Italian honey
123 Sip
125 Love personified
127 Blockhead
128 In-flight info, in brief
129 Soft shoes
133 Yankee's club
134 67-Down, for one
136 Peak in les Alpes
137 Biology lab organism
139 "Hogwash!"
140 Kyrgyzstan range
141 One who hasn't turned pro?
142 "The Sterile Cuckoo" actress, 1969
143 French 101 infinitive
144 Corn cake
145 Enlisted V.I.P.'s
146 9:59
147 Ph.D.'s work: Abbr.
148 Sugar lovers
149 Lake Erie-to-Lake Ontario dir.

Dec/Jan

s	m	t	w	t	f	s
					1	2
3	4	5	6	7	8	9
10	11	12	13	14	15	16
17	18	19	20	21	22	23
24	25	26	27	28	29	30
31						

JANUARY

BOXING DAY OBSERVED (CANADA, UK)   *monday*

28 362

tuesday

29 363

wednesday

30 364

thursday

○ **31** 365

NEW YEAR'S DAY   *friday*

1 1

saturday

2 2

sunday

3 3

1. SHUFFLING FEAT

```
JONES   PRAGMATIC   FOGS
ADIEU LITTLENELL   ONIT
YELLEDATELATELY    REVE
   DOT   ADE   DAFTER
INTERVIEWSSTEVEIRWIN
ATEE   INN   ICE  NEONS
MEATHEADSMADEHASTE
ARREAR   ONAROLL   RUB
   VOA  BOND   ENGINE
VIDEOSTOREOVERDOESIT
MANON  PAR  IDA  GRETA
OPPRESSINGPOPSINGERS
YOUARE   MOPS   DOI
ART  AVERAGE   UNCLES
   HOMESINONMOONSHINE
OFWAY  RAE  AIM  AROW
GRAVELYILLVALLEYGIRL
RIVERA   EIN   NEE
EVEN SNAKEBITBEATNIKS
SOTO SOLORECORD  ATRIA
SLOT  EMPHYSEMA  THEAX
```

2. MATCH PLAY

```
   CON   CENT   RAY  SHIN
PALO  TAXCO  PELE  STAPH
AMOF  AGGRAVATOR   ERROL
SERAGLIO   STUN   AXED
OLDTELEVISIONGAMESHOW
   SYR  DOGIE   MASSEUR
ASSET   FAUNS  WIZ  TATE
PICK  CHIRP  STEEPEDIN
ATOE  FORESAILS   ESSES
CAPSULES   LSU   APPT
ERE   PARTSOFAREBUS
   GETS  ARI  BOLIVIAN
ESSEN   ANCESTORS  ABIT
NOTONHAND  PEACE   SISS
ONIT  EST  SAINT  MEATY
RICHARD   TERRA   EPA
MAKEROFTHEHOMEVERSION
   BRED  ERMA  VERTICAL
MIAMI  KNOTTYPINE  SAKE
MILAN  ATWO  OATES  AMIR
MILL   TON   BRAD   LEE
```

3. NAME DROPPING

```
SCAB  DATES  CPAS  EWING
POLE  IWILL  OAHU  SONAR
AMERICASMOSTWAN   PESTO
SEVENTY  OPTS   SMASHUP
MTETNA  BRER  TOEIN  ARE
SOLTI  PRESIDENTIALPAR
   AEIOU   PARIS   EELS
EAT   ALIAS  SRO  GEE
GREATMINDSTHINKAL  TPS
GIRTH   SIGH   SAGAMORE
COCAINE  ATARI  LATERON
USEDCARS   NANA   ERASE
POL  KENTUCKYFRIEDCHIC
   RES  ADO  SOILS  STA
SPAT   CLINT   GILDS
HAVEACHANGEOFHE   INSET
ELI   SIEGE  SNIT  STATUE
COASTAL   GLEN  TOSPARE
ROTOR  SOFTASABABYSBOT
AKELA  ELIO  ELITE  ALPE
BADDY  ADES  CEDAR  TEAR
```

4. HITTING THE SAUCE

```
STARSHIP   EMUS  GROOVED
SEMOLINA   LOST  LEONINE
TEACADDY  FREESOYPARTY
   KEITH   ANNUM   RTS
AIOLIHAVEEYESFORYOU
ROMANO   NEST   INOIL
OWING   HANG   TOPLESS
MATE  TABASCOSMOKE  NOT
ANS  DOZES  OREO  ONLY
   GAGA  SWILLS  GRUEL
HOMEFORTHEHOLLANDAISE
APART   DEADEN   BAAL
VENT  CHAR  QUERY  MAD
ORE  CASHANDCURRY  JIMI
CATCHIT  HENS   VIXEN
   REDAS  SRAS  PAVING
WERETHEPESTOFFRIENDS
LEA   EERIE   SOLON
TEETERTARTAR  MOVEAWAY
ADDENDA   IERE  PRESSONE
BASSSAX   SSNS  HASTINGS
```

5. THE FRENCH CONNECTION

```
AZALEA  ALABAMA  MILSAP
RETIES  SOMINEX  ONEIDA
PROVES  SWINGSETMISSES
ONE  ARE   EASE   THINS
HEADSETTAILS   ASIA
HOSTESS  ARMS   CANTBE
SUB  SITATOP  HASAT  IRV
TREK  NOSES  BOLERO  CIA
   CRU  CARETDRIVER  KON
DIKES  KPS  EASTER  RECD
ICEBAG   ANY   SEETHE
VATS  LACTIC  JLO  WAFER
INC  BALLETCHAIN   ELL
NSA  EZPASS  UNMAN  MEOW
EEL  LIONS  TRIEDON  AVE
DELETE   BLOC  ALIASES
   SSRS  ROCKETROLLER
WAIST  LEAH   REN   NAH
UNDERLOCKETKEY  GUISES
SEENAT  REMAINS  ESCORT
SWEEPS  USEDPOT  ROONEY
```

6. ALL IN THE PAST

```
OLAV  APSE  AUTISM  CUR
PUNCHLINES  TRICIA  ANY
EXTRACTORTRAILERS  LTD
SEESTO  WOUK  TAUT  LIE
   STDS  COLEEXPORTER
ANDS  TRUCK  ETRE  DUH
PEACE  AIL  GETS  ONEAL
EXLAXATTITUDE  MONOCLE
TEMPI   NESS  LIV  NOLO
   PER  MIST  AIRES  POS
QUICKEXCHANGEARTIST
PUN  TIKIS  TOON  TIC
AIDE  SEV  COEN  AMANA
SEERESS  GARLICEXPRESS
STRIP  CARY  SHA  YULES
   SKI  MRED  STATE  SLAW
EXPATPAULSEN   TADS
NEE  HIND  LOIS  GOBACK
ANN  EXTENSIONHEADACHE
MOD  TILSIT  PROTRACTOR
INS  SEETHE  EWES  HEWN
```

7. NEW AR-RANGEMENTS

```
C O H O S T   A G N A T E     P A T R O N
A V A N T I   D R I V E R   E S S E N C E
R E V E A L   D I N I N G A L A C R A T E
A R E A L   M O S T       W A T E R
F R A M E R I N T H E D E L L   N O R S E
E A N   R E N       G A D   S T R O L L
N E D   A G A M E O F D R A T S   L A S
    R A S P   B I N   T I E T O   E L L E
I P A N A   E A S T   E C O N   D I O
D E F E N D S   O U R S   A N I   O N M E
O R O   G O T O W R A P S P E E D   G I A
S E R A   S E N   E D I T   D R A G O N S
G M T   A R A P   E D E R   R O U G E
A R U M   G O L E M   E L I   A N E T
S I S   W E L L R E G R A D E D   S T D
A N I M A S   I R A   G A O   H E F
P E C O S   I L L E G A L R A M S D E A L
R H I N O       B E A N   M E T R O
P R A T I N G C O M P A N Y   S O U R E R
C O R O N A E   P R E S T O   E N C A S E
S T I N G S     S I P H O N   A D E P T S
```

8. CELEBRATION

```
G U E S T F E E S   S A D E   A B B O T T
A N A H E I M C A   C R I T   G O A L I E
P I R A T E S O F T H E C A R I B B E A N
    P O L   E B O O K   I N S O
T E N D E R   A O L E R S   L O A M S
R I I S   W E B   L A N C E   E N R O L
E N V   E X E C U T E   S A T E D   T U O
I N O R D E R   S E R B   O R D   L S T
C O L O N S   I F S   A I G   G E N I E
E V I T A   F R A T   B R E T   R A N K
S E G A   H A R I   Y E A H   S K E W
N A R D   A T E E   F A D E   M A L T A
T R Y I T   E S S   O D E   E I L E E N
B I D   S O O   T R O Y   W R E S T E D
R O E   N O T E R   A D O R E R S   T R A
A N N E E   T R E V I   U A R   M E S S
E S S A Y   A I D I N G   M E S M E R
    S L A W   Z E L I G   W I T
I N D I A N A J O N E S A D V E N T U R E
T A L E N T   I N N S   O N E D O L L A R
T H I R D S   B E A S   L A T E T E E N S
```

9. A LOT OF CHOICES

```
E L E C T R A   O L E G   E M I S S I V E
S A M O Y E D   N O T A   A C T U A T E D
S U B U R B A N B L A Z E R V E N T U R E
O D O R   A B A R   L E M   R O P E R
    S W I G   R E A   B I G H A I R
    C I V I C A C C O R D I N S I G H T
H E W   J I G   K O O   S A T I E   O I D
U T E   O S L O   M U S   N I L   B V D S
S A B L E C O U G A R M Y S T I Q U E
T O B E   O I L   T E A K   N O R R I S
L I E N O R S   A N S E L   M E M E N T O
E N D O R A   B R A Y   T I A   A M I N
F R O N T I E R S T A N Z A Q U E S T
E P E E   L A P   A T O   N O V A   N S A
L I E   V A L E T   E S L   L I T   T O G
I N T R E P I D R A M C A R A V A N
I T S A S I N   A S A   R O B O
B U B B E   M O M   A R E A   J U N O
E S C O R T M U S T A N G E X P L O R E R
R E D S A U C E   C Y A N   P E E K S A T
G R E E N B A Y   H O Y A   O R D E A L S
```

10. PUZZLED EXPRESSION

```
U M P S   P A V A R O T T I   F A L L
C E R T   O V U L A T I O N   I L E A
S T O O P   K E E P S A T I T   O S I E R
D E S P I S E R   S H Y   L E A T H E R S
R A P P O R T S     M E R S E N N E
S M I L E Y☺   H O R D E   ☺ C R E A M S
P A C E R S   M I N I O N S   H O T T I E
C I A   E N R O U T E   O C T
A D L I B   S W E A T B A N D   L A R K S
N O P E   S M E L L   I R O N
C O W S L I P   P R Y   D U S T B I N
E V E   D A T A   R I D E   E N E
D E I   ☺ F A C T S   F U N N Y ☺   L T R
E R G S   H I C C U P S   B L E D
W H I T E ☺   M A U L S   ☺ S A V E R
H A T C H E T ☺   R E L   ☺ P O W D E R S
O T T   C L O C K ☺   ☺ V A L U E   P A N
B E R G   S W A M   A N A P   C O C A
B R A I D   E R A S   S S G T   F A Q I R
L E I L A   L D R S   T E L E   U S U A L
E D N A S   S S T S   U S E S   R E E L S
```

11. YOU ARE HERE

```
A T T A C H E   P E N P A L   C A P G U N
B O O S T E R   E M E R G E   A R I O S O
U R B A N D E O D O R A N T   R I P S A W
S E A N   B A R   W E B P A G E S
E R G   N E U R O C O N S E R V A T I V E
D O O D A D S   A L S   E A T   P E T
E N E   M O P E   K E Y N O T E R S
T H E C U R R Y I N G G A M E   E R A
A U R A   E E L   O U T R A G E
E N O L A G A Y   S H E A   M E N S C H
L C D   B U R E A U B R I D G E S   H O O
S H E I L A   P R O S   F A S T T A L K
P E R C A L E   A L I   O K I E
M S S   H O U R L Y M A T R I M O N Y
C O L O N I A L S   S E A T   O N E
O N O   O C S   J A L   N U D I S T S
T O W N W I T H O U T P U R I T Y   O O H
P I O N E E R S   S I P   S L U E
M E A G R E   A L T E R E D S T A T U R E
A C C E S S   L O S E T O   A E R A T E D
S T E R E S   S P O K E N   T R A G E D Y
```

12. LIGHTEN UP

```
R E C T   A R T I S T   S K I D   J A W
L O B A R   J E A N I E   T Y R O   U T E
A M E R I C A N P I N K C R O S S   L O I
P E R P L E X E S   H U T   P I N G
D O T E L L   W I L L I A M O F P E A C H
I T I   N O E N D   O U N C E S
S E T P O I N T   A E C   O G R I S H
L E M O N C R E A M J A C K E T S   I O U
E R A S   E N V   E S T   S I L O S
D O N T G O   S A L M O N   M A A N D P A
M I S T E R M I N T J E A N S
P A L A V E R   I N D I R A   A T H A N D
S C O N E   O T C   A V A   O L E O
S U V   A Z U R E C O L L A R W O R K E R
E R R A T A   C M A   S P E C T A T E
I N P A I N   T I A R A   S S T
M O O D P E R I W I N K L E   T A M A R A
P O T S   E N O   I R R I G A T E S
I D I   U L T R A L A V E N D E R R A Y S
S L O   P E R U   U R A N I A   A G L E T
H E N   C O O N   V E R S E S   M E L S
```

13. THE MAMAS AND THE PAPAS

```
ACME  ARCA  CZAR  ATBEST
SLAPSDOWN  HUTU  LARDER
PARACHUTEPANTS  BRIDLE
ISR  HOG  MARINEMAMMALS
CHIT  CHAIS        RNA
     AHI  PASTPARTICIPLE
AGENDAS  IWERE  ASSAIL
ADELAIDE  VITALE  ACNE
DAMASKS  MASSMARKETING
ABASH  BUTT  PLEX  FEY
THESTAGE  MASERATI
ESE  LEEK  PARE  MOCHA
PARALLELPARKS  TOPSPIN
SNIP  MARCIE  HALLPASS
OKAPIS  VIRAL  ORDEALS
MALLMANAGEMENT  SRI
ARI  VOLGA  ESSE
PAJAMAPARTIES  RUE  ATM
LIONEL  MAYFLOWERMADAM
ODENSE  ISPS  AABATTERY
TALESE  SHOO  PRES  ASKS
```

14. PLACEMENT TEST

```
TATARS  SONATA  HMO  GEORG
OMELET  ARAGON  URI  RIVER
NEXTTONOTHING  NIL  ARENA
STERNO  STYES  LATERON
REEDS  ADLER  ALI  HUT
DIANA  HASTO  AIRMAN  ANE
ATBAT  FOLLOWINGUP  PUCE
DUCT  OLEGS  NCOS  TOILES
APSE  PARE  AFTERSHAVE
KEG  RETRO  IMPARTED
LIFTING  IRAE  PEAS  CONE
IDLERS  AMNESIC  BRETON
MOON  ETNA  MMES  TASSELS
ALPACINO  FAUST  ART
BEFORELONG  ACHE  ZETA
SCULLS  APER  STOOD  ALAS
ORNE  AHEADOFTIME  EPOCH
LID  SENSES  PLACE  LANKY
OTE  PEG  SERIO  ROGET
MERRILL  SONOF  REMISS
ORDER  EGO  BESIDEONESELF
NIOBE  REX  ORISON  UNTRUE
SAGAS  SEX  TSETSE  STATED
```

15. SPEAKING CANADIAN

```
BRAG  DEBUG  CASK  CPAS
LUEGO  AROSE  ALEE  RODE
ISLEOFMANET  YANG  ILEX
NIA  APSE  SCENT  ITISI
DEPRESSED  TAN  RACISTS
ASSENT  JOHNNYCACHET
STENT  FETE  NEE  UMA
ROLAIDS  PATELLA
SHAY  PERSIANLAME  MATT
HONOREES  LAYLA  HASTA
ARGUED  ALINE  LISTEN
DROVE  CAPON  AMASSING
YORE  HYDEPARQUET  ENDO
RAGDOLL  SAUNTER
ORA  ASS  NOTE  OMITS
DOCTORFILLET  MARNIE
ALAMODE  AIL  STAIRSTEP
REBEL  LENTO  MADE  ORT
RAIL  CLAD  POISONPENNE
ERNE  HOSE  ENTER  FLEET
NYSE  EWER  DEERE  CODY
```

16. MAKING A LEFT

```
GOOGLE  ROUST  LAURA
PUTRID  EQUATION  ENRON
ARTIFICIALRESPIRATION
DETENTES  TIGERS
OVO  NOES  MECHANICAL
NIPPER  THEFIRST  ELLA
ATEAT  WEANED  GUNROOM
LARDS  WINCE  CLOSE  DUB
AMA  KINDA  MAEWEST
BITMAP  SYMBOLIN  SHIRT
ENOUGH  PAT  LIENEE
LARGE  TOGETONA  YENFOR
SOBERED  RIFLE  ORR
MBA  LOREN  VOTRE  MARIA
EARLDOM  PILEIN  OLMEC
SINE  POORMARK  INSANE
HOOTENANNY  AINT  LTD
DRAPES  DEPARTED
MAJORMEDICALINSURANCE
CROWE  RATIFIES  REHEAL
SPEND  YEATS  NYLONS
```

Note: The shaded squares spell L-E-F-T.

17. CRY ME A RIVER

```
DNA  LUSH  SLEW  METTLE
RUG  ASSET  PARE  ALOHAS
ODERINTHECOURT  REDACT
LINED  SHROUDS  RICOTTA
LETSBE  ERNS  MINT  OAT
CANIHAVESOMME  NITE
MATURED  SADLY  WISE
TEHEE  SOFA  SEX  TETE
GRAM  LORDHAVEMERSEY
MEG  HINGE  BAZOOKA
SHE  AVONTOBEALONE  GEM
NOSTRIL  UNMAN  RRR
LETSGOYANGTZES  OOPS
HALL  GIN  OXEN  HUSSY
GERE  SONAR  ONASSIS
SUBS  GOGETEMTIGRIS
TAR  RELO  BURN  ARENAS
ONEFOLD  DIECAST  DAILY
LIAISE  CATCHMEIFYUKON
INKJET  ALEC  SADIE  ONO
DESIST  PIMA  MENS  NED
```

18. ALL IN

```
MASTER  ICUS  OPT  DRAKE
OCTANE  SPRAINED  RELET
SHALLOWBUSINESS  IDLES
EON  PAN  ANDIE  UPDOS
YODELER  TINTER  AWHO
DONTHAVEACALLOWMAN
SCAGGS  UPI  HSI  ANENT
CERES  ALPACA  HST
ACTSO  BALLADMOUTHING
REF  NAB  RISE  ESPIES
FLIT  WALLETNURSE  SRTA
SILICA  ETYM  UPN  VAL
AMERICASCALLUP  ORATE
ETA  KNEELS  PANAM
MEADE  RTS  NNE  GROANS
IMDALLYINGTOSEEYOU
GAMY  OSCARS  EMBLEMS
NIGEL  TRITT  MOC  PEA
CURAD  BALLROOMCLOSETS
SEEME  SCALABLE  UNSERS
ALDEN  AST  PEDS  BASSEY
```

19. ONE FOR THE BOOKS

```
S N U F F   C A T E R   E P S   N E I L
T A P I R   U T I L E   R A T   O N M E
B R I D G E T J 1 S S D I A R Y   F R A G
R E L O   E N O S   A T T N   L O G O
E A T   I S T   T H E L O V E L Y B 1 S
A K I N D   W U H A N   E Z E R
M Y P O I N T A N D I D O H A V E 1
  S O N I C E   L I T E R A L   G A S
L 1 S O M E D O V E   S E A R L E   E V A
A L I A S   E G G   R O L E   L A Y
L I M P   T H E N O S P I N Z 1   D A L I
A N I   B O O R   A R F   S E T O N
L E A   A T R I S K   1 T R U E T H I N G
A R N   R E S C U E S   H A S B R O
A N D T H E N T H E R E W E R E N 1
U R D U   D E A N E   E N N E A
A R O O M O F 1 S O W N   C A P   C O D
T S A R   L I S P   I V A N   R O N A
B U R N   M E T A L K P R E T T Y 1 D A Y
A L E E   E R E   A F R O S   I S L E T
Y A R D   C O P   S C E N T   C L Y D E
```

20. E · IE, IO

```
M O P E D   O N E S E C   G I R L   M R I
O C U L I   R E C A L L   A D I A   Y E N
B A L L E T B A R R I O   P L A Y G O L F
I N L E T S   T U G   S W E E T I E P I E
L A T S   H R E   T E E   A N T I C S
E D A   Z I O N M A S T E R S   T O A S T
  A B S O R B   E L K S   A L O O F
T O T E B A G   A H A B   F L A P
S L A M   R O L A I D S   B E R M U D A
S P A T   G T O   R O T E   R A Y G U N
C U R I O F O R T H E C O M M O N C O L D
A R I O S O   S E A N   B A N   A S T A
L O A N E R S   S T E P D A D   P S I S
A N T I   C P A S   L O R E L E I
  S T E E L   R E E L   F A N O U T
A N G L O   C A M E R A L I O N S   S O T
M O R A Y S   O D E   A R D   S H A H
E V E N S T E V E N   F O G   R A T E D R
L E A D R O L E   O L D G R A Y M A R I O
I N T   U N I T   S A I L E D   A L I E N
A A S   S E A S   E X C E E D   T E N S E
```

21. ALTERNATING CURRENT

```
C A P R A   S A B O T   A T M S   R E A P
O S I E R   P I A N O   C R O C   E A S E
M A T T E   I D L E R   H A M O F F R Y E
O N H A N D R E M A R K   P A R A L L E L
    L A U E R   L E N A   C R O
T A O I S M   F L Y O F F T H E W A L L
A R I A   A L I I   B R E W E D   R E A
R E N T S   A T R I A   W A R   S I A M
T A K E O N T H E G L O V E S   B L A D E
  C I T E   N A D I R   S E I N E S
M A N A C L E   P O S E D   F E R M E N T
A B A S E S   F O R K S   E R L E
N O S I R   R E L E A S E D O F F B A I L
I L S A   H I D   N A K E D   T R I P E
A L A   S O C I A L   E N O L   A L S O
C A U G H T O N G U A R D   O R I S O N
R A W   E R N O   S W A I N
D E S O L A T E   K N O C K O F F W O O D
O N P U T T I N G   A M E E R   L A R V A
N Y E T   E D I T   L I N E D   E S S E N
S A W S   R E D O   S E T T S   S H O N E
```

22. FIELD OF DREAMS

```
S O B E R S   L A K M E   A G E L I N E
A L A N O N   O N I O N   C O L A N U T
F I N D S A B O T T L E O N A B E A C H
A V I   S K I P I T   L E D A   B L E U
R E S T   I N E   E D G E   D O E R S
I S H A L L G R A N T Y O U O N E W I S H
  R A Y   L I S P   S P U N
A S T I   L O O S   F E E L   P S A S
P E A C E I N T H E M I D D L E E A S T
R O A N   L S U   L A V   R A N T O
E L F   A M A P O F T H E A R E A   J I G
P O E S Y   P R O   C U R   F O G Y
I G R A N T Y O U A N O T H E R W I S H
N Y N Y   R E M S   U B E R   A B E T
  G I A N   P I T A   U K E
T H E C U B S I N A W O R L D S E R I E S
H O U R S   A S O F   O O H   S N A P
O L G A   D I N T   D O G N A P   T S E
L E T M E S E E T H A T M A P A G A I N
O N E I L L S   L A T T E   E V O K E D
W E S T I E S   C L E O N   D E T E R S
```

23. HALLOWEEN PLAY

```
S A L U T E   C U L T   S O D D E N
P R E S E N T   B R I E F S   S P R U C E
I N T E N S I V E S C A R E   S P O T O N
N O T D O   B A R A   B A N S   O N C L E
  R A I N   K A P O W   N E H
C A S A   M A S K I N G P R I C E   C I E
A T P L A Y   E L I S E   P A N D O R A
C H I L L S T R E E T   B E N T O V E R
H O R O L   R E P S   P L U S   J E S T
E S O T E R I C   T A O S   I S O N T O
  G A M E S H O W G H O S T
C A C H E T   I S U P   H U R R A H E D
O B O E   U V E A   B M O C   A M O C O
B E L L R O P E   F R I G H T F I E L D
O L D D E A R   E E L E R   R E D R A G
L E S   B R O O M S E R V I C E   E S T E
  C D E   A B I T E   L A Y S
M O R E L   R E N I   I M I N   A P S E S
O T E L L O   S E V E N Y E A R W I T C H
W H A L E R   E M A I L S   L E T T U C E
N O M A D S   L S A T   M O A N E D
```

24. POUNDING THE PAVEMENT

```
B I O L A B   S N O B   C A S H   E F S
I G N O R E   A U R A   A S T I   D O W D
C O E R C E   A M A N   L E A N   S U E R
T H E S T A T E N I S L A N D F E R R Y
E C O N   N C R   S K I   I L O V E
T H U   M A N H A T T A N T R A N S F E R
C A R R O L   I L I E   O N U S
O W E S   G R I N S A T   I R E
A B R O N X T A L E   G I S   E N N E A D
R E E F   O R O   D O C   T U R I S M O
R U N T H E N E W Y O R K M A R A T H O N
A L E R T L Y   E A T   J A M   S O N G
S A G E S T   S L Y   P R O M Q U E E N S
H E E   O O H L A L A   I T L L
O R E O   A R C O   R E F I T S
F I V E B O R O U G H C O U R S E   N O S
E N E R O   N E D   N T H   A A R E
A T R E E G R O W S I N B R O O K L Y N
T O O N   L E V I   D O R A   A E G E A N
S I N O   A P E S   A G I N   K N E A D S
T A W   D O N E   H O O K   S O R R O W
```

25. FLYING START

```
JAMESFOX   TILLAGE   QTRS
ADAMSALE   AMOEBAE   WRAP
NORTHWESTPASSAGE    EAVE
IRT  AKA   AIRES   ARLEN
SNIPPET   UNITEDWESTAND
      RESEAT   OREILLY
JAPED  BEDE   STLO   SHE
IHOP  AMERICANCHOPSUEY
GEL  SPAY   PORT   EARLE
SMELLARAT  LIESTO   RPMS
   VIRGINWOOLSWEATER
LIAM  EATING  TIPTOEING
ETUIS   COIF   NEET   SOO
DELTABLUESSINGER   LEVI
AMT  LIEN   TROI   AIDAN
   ALFATAH   OTITIS
SONGOFSOLOMON  MRMAGOO
OXBOW  ELENA   POE   ERN
LIAR  CONTINENTALDRIFT
ODEA   PROTEAN  ALLATSEA
SERE   ROBERTO  RESTSTOP
```

26. BLUE STREAK

```
ALL*S   TRIB   SCRAM   LOAD
VIOLA   OONA   THERE   UNDO
APRIL   BYFITS&*TS   T&EM
SPENT   EARTH   LEIS   HOPE
TINGED   LOSE   EASEMENTS
      DIGIN   SIR   TSAR
CWT   MIST   ERS   RANTO
PLEASANT   TVA   PAGIN@ED
H&LING   IRE   BITES   ILE
DELLA   ADMEN   REEL   NOES
STOPTHE#@%*&CUSSING
STIR   WOKE   STEEP   HEWED
TIM   AILED   OLD   PACINO
UNEARNED   OLE   SHAREDIN
BEDIM   STU   CHAN   SEC
   ROAD   ITT   REMIT
#STERLING   ICED   CENSES
C&ID   CAIN   OR@ED   NAOMI
AIDA   ALTERN@IVE   %ILES
KEEL   PERRY   EVIL   EVENS
ERSE   PROSE   SELL   REDDY
```

27. REJECTED COLLEGE MASCOTS

```
BRAGS   ADELA   IPOD   JESTS
PIEMAN   LUMEN   MERE   UPTON
ULTIMO   EMBODIMENT   GIJOE
SKIDMOREBANANAPEEL   SOLE
SENSATE   BRA   CCS   REACHER
ERAT   LAE   RAU   SECONDS
SSE   SEAPLANE   LEE   RIPS
NAVYBLUEBLAZER   DAWNS
BYGONES   SWASTIKAS   LOON
LEADEN   BASE   DEO   GPO   RNA
TATI   OAFISH   BLACKTOP
COLGATETOOTHPASTE
LIBELERS   DRAGON   ESSE
ORR   ANI   WOO   ARTE   TOPTEN
LAOS   ASCENDANT   POPEYED
LEWIS   HUNTERGATHERER
NDAK   ETH   TERRAPIN   PCS
LABELED   ELY   YDS   CLAP
AMASSER   PLO   ORT   ISRAELI
REGT   NOTREDAMEHUNCHBACK
INGER   WEAVESAWEB   ROADIE
ADEPT   SADE   ANOSE   INLETS
TERSE   ETAL   PINER   MEADE
```

28. HIGH JINKS

```
RABBIT   COMESTO   SCALD
ELLERY   SHRAPNEL   ELDER
TAILOR   HIGHTOPSOCIETY
AMMAN   SERA   BEER   MAMA
POPTOPWARNER   ENNOBLED
   ERRORS   GEE   APE
REDDEER   BOXTOPTURTLE
OUR   ZEBRAS   TRUES   VAT
ALAST   MIS   GAIL   IROC
RAGTOPPICKER   SLAPDASH
   SARAH   HELIO   UBOLT
GOTRIDOF   TIPTOPONEILL
INRE   NOUS   PIS   ERNIE
LEI   SUERS   JESUIT   GMS
LAPTOPDANCER   HOLYSEE
   ORT   AUD   SPORES
SHOWBOAT   BIGTOPKAHUNA
YARN   IDYL   RALE   RAKES
BLACKTOPBEAUTY   INPAWN
ILLAT   BEAMMEUP   SEESTO
LEERS   EARFULS   ODDEST
```

29. THE OTHER HALF

```
CARR   BLEAK   BESS   ITCH
OLIO   EARTH   KUBLA   NORA
HINTSFROMABELARD   SWAT
NEGATORS   TANGY   DOINGS
   TORY   MARNE   NEAT
ALCOVE   NIMOY   CONFUSED
DEARE   DININGOATES   TAI
DAMS   PRES   ARID   TERM
ESP   BLACKWESSON   LIENS
REGULATE   ADHEM   RUMPS
   OBITS   MYERS   MOREL
FLOSS   LAINE   PANCREAS
ALIAS   BURNSWRENCH   JLO
GOAT   PANG   OREO   TIER
RAT   RAGGEDYAMOS   CALVE
ATHLETES   RELET   WHILES
   OPEL   DIALS   TEAL
ACTION   GENRE   ORANGISH
LOUT   THANKSGIVINGADAM
MUTE   EASTS   ELATE   TORO
SPUR   DIPS   DELED   ELIS
```

30. YOU WILL BE MISSED

```
MANIC   LEAF   OLGA   SERFS
ARENA   ERGO   BOON   ASORT
SCOTMASTER   LANDRYSOAP
HON   ELSE   EZINE   ANOMIE
   SLOE   STAG   OHNO   MDT
JEWELERSLOPE   NEG   LANE
OTITIS   OYL   ROTATOR
TESSA   COLDWATERFACETS
DRE   MANY   OLEG   FIT
ONO   MAP   TRIAGE   WICCA
WANDEREDLONELYASACLOD
NLERS   KEENON   TIN   ELM
   ISO   COIF   APEX   ALI
AFTERNOONOFAFAN   DINER
TRESSED   SIN   RENEGE
TENT   LIZ   AHOSEDIVIDED
EDS   LINE   DENT   EDIT
METEOR   PHONE   GAGA   KEY
PRODFATHER   MAIDENANTS
TINEA   EYRE   ARAL   CHORE
SCENT   TROD   NYNY   ESTER
```

31. THE REFEREE OF ROMANCE

```
SLID  SWAM  CAFE  █ LACED
HOME  URSA  AGRA  BORAXO
OVAL  PASSINTERFERENCE
TEXAS PEABO ADLAI  VET
  YEP SLAP  KROC   RASH
UNNECESSARYROUGHNESS
NOODLES        YUM  HED
PROCURER  STAT PERUSES
CANADA  EATON  DEADBALL
  LET CLAP  SAND  HBO
AXELS FAIRCATCH  BFLAT
RED   HOST  OMAR  BAA
KNOCKOUT MAMBO ALCOVE
SAMHILL  AUTO  NAILEDIN
  ITY ADS   STYMIED
ILLEGALUSEOFTHEHANDS
ICAL  HULL  CRUE  DOS
LEW GODOT HEDDA  OKIES
OFFENSIVEHOLDING  IDLE
NOUGAT  ERIE LUTE  NOME
AGLOW  RYES EMIT  GLOP
```

32. GRIDIRON GLOSSARY

```
BYTWO  TUBED  BBC   ALAN
BORON  AMATI  BLOODLINE
QUARTERBACK  OURSELVES
IRONORE   ABED  CARAT
DENY  STADIUMBLEACHERS
RRR HES   GRAYAREA
ANITA   SHAG   WES  RIDS
WIDERECEIVERS  ROMANIA
SEEA  DANCE  EKE  PUNIER
  MAGI  MAULS  SANTA
NUMBERONEDRAFTPICKS
VENAL  OPENS  ORCA
EASTER  TRU  FABLE  BPOE
STEERED  OFFENSIVELINE
TOTS  SOS  UVEA  LEPER
  TITMOUSE  STS  III
PASSINTERFERENCE  ANNE
UDALL  OLEO  BOOTLEG
RELATEDTO  THEUPRIGHTS
SNOWSHOES  WORSE  FIORD
EONS  STD  ANTES  ESTES
```

33. NO MORE ACHES

```
SAD  NIPS   IMARI  FLOPS
ANALOGUE  IRONED  AUDIO
MANITOBA  SALTLICKCITY
BICKERSTREET  ORIENTS
ALEE   TEE   TATERS
  AKELA  BOOKIES  WAD
MRS  GIVEMEABRICK  JIMI
CENSURE   USEIN  SOCIO
CNOTES  CPR   STREAKER
LEWIS  CHEERUP  OMANI
WFL QUICKEROATS  MSS
  LETUS  SASSERS  PILED
BLITHEST   UMA  PIRATE
LACTO  USUAL  LACONIC
ELKO  BIRTHDAYKICK  DNA
DOS  AIRBASE  AIDES
  BUNION  ELL   APES
BOARDED  SIRLOINSTICK
UNDERTICKING  TOETOTOE
SCONE  UPENDS  ONEONONE
TESTY  MANGO  NADA  NOT
```

34. "NATIONAL" HOLIDAY

```
RIFTS  ELMS   FLARE  HAVE
ALLAH  TOOT   LAVER  OMEN
YOUREGHANABUYAFATBIRD
ROOF  KRIS   HORSE
SOFFITS  READ  CARESSED
UPLIFT  AEON  SHOAT
STUFFANDPUTITINJAPAN
HIKES  EMIT  DICE  EPOS
ICES   TWIN  TITO  SATIRE
  BEER  KROC  CALISTA
TAIWANLEGWITHTHEOTHER
ALMONDS  RATS  RANT
LOAVES  CONE  FINS  GRIT
LUGE   CRUZ  SLUG  PEEVE
DONOTLETANYONERUSSIA
DROPS  IRAE  UNTIES
BACKDATE  SKIT  LICENSE
ENROL   SOON  PANT
FEEDYOURHUNGARYGUESTS
IAMA  UNION  EVIL  ALOHA
TREK  ROPED  SEGA  LINED
```

35. FLORIDA KEY

```
PGS   FEB   IAM   POMADE
DOES  OLESTRA  PERCALES
QUAKERFLOATS  AGITATES
BASALT  FLYCHROMOSOME
ACC  KEEPTO  OISE
CHASE  SHY  TSPS  SITTER
HELP  ETA  SKIPIT  SHULA
LETTERSTODEARFLABBY
TWOCAR  AIR  ERNIE  TEAS
REPINE  ONUS  PUBS
ESSAY  PHOTOFLOP  INFER
LAME  LIAR  OTOOLE
EAST  IAMBI  LII  REJOIN
TOSEA  LILITH  LES  KIRK
SEESTO  NATE  BET  MESON
WALT  TOSSER  HBO
FLORALHISTORY  LIANES
LIMABEAN  HEADFLUSHERS
ANISETTE  ADDSALT  ASTO
WATERS   ISE   ABE  SAS
```

36. FROM THE PRESIDENTIAL RECORD BOOKS

```
LOON  ALA  IBIZA  STOLE
ETNA  MARKTWAIN  BOREAL
WITHOUTSAYINGTHEWORDI
DOH  FSTOP   SEABED
ESE  TEEN  ASP  SLOT TLC
REFEEDS  WILLI  EPOCHAL
OVA  JAMAICAN  REBA
ADUE  CHER  TEEM  SHIMON
TURN  RAFFLES  EQUATOR
EMTS  UNFAIR  DRUBS  NUS
ABHOR  SERT  DIII  HORNE
TWO  ADORE  MUSCLY  GOIN
AFFIRMS  CANTATA  LEON
GIJANE  OOHS  ONSO  EDNA
ETUI  ANTIHERO  PRO
SELLERS  CLINT  FRESCOS
TRY  MITT  LED  FLEA  TUM
SECRET  PRESS  RTE
WROTEAONESENTENCEWILL
VANERN  SAMMYSOSA  ANET
ADAMS  ERASE  NEN  GETS
```

37. YEARS ON END

```
WHIRR . DMITRI . OPERAHAT
OOZED . IAMBIC . REDIVIDE
WHATAMESSAGE . ELICITOR
SOAS . ASS . ATHLETE . CBS
. SKIER . ESC . EASE . GHEE
. NAVYYARDAGE . PERI .
DCAREA . WEISS . AIRINGS
HOH . FLOUTED . EGGINGON
AREOLA . POPUPADAGE . PRO
LACTATED . PARITY . LOEB
. KOP . ARID . LIFE . TIS .
ANTS . TRADES . ISTHATSO
NEH . HOTFOOTAGE . HERALD
TWILIGHT . ONADARE . GUS
ITSOKAY . ASPIN . REDDER
. OWES . BUMSTEERAGE .
PIUS . TATA . AFL . DECAF
ORT . ATALOSS . DEE . IMAX
SEARCHME . HOOVERDAMAGE
ENGINEER . ENTERS . RANIN
DEEPENDS . DETEST . PLANA
```

38. AT THE PRESENT TIME

```
SATRAP . BRITISH . AWAKED
EQUATE . SAVANNA . SALAMI
CUTTHEPAPERFOLDANDTIE
TASSELS . PARLE . TOOTS
. NET . SHONE . AHA .
BALLAD . GLINT . TRADUCED
ODIE . SHIN . SHED . SOLA
SENTENCEDTOTHISJOBAMI
OLD . NOONE . BRANT . VASES
MAY . SLOT . PLANK . ENTRY
. GNAT . CRIME . LARK .
BELLA . SLOGS . GALA . ADZ
ONAIR . STOWE . PERIL . CEE
WONDERCOULDALEGALCHAP
ECCE . HAUT . NINE . HELP
SHERBERT . HANNA . USEDTO
. YAP . LEROY . ATE .
AHEAP . ISOLA . CANTONS
FINDAWAYTOBEATTHEWRAP
AROUSE . NUTLIKE . ACACIA
NEWEST . ESSENCE . NASALS
```

39. WHAT PEOPLE MIGHT SAY BEFORE DOING THIS PUZZLE

```
SCAMPI . TRIODE . SECANT
NOPAIN . OUTBOX . ARAPAHO
ICANSPAREEIGHTMINUTES
PORK . IBARS . TOILET . IFS
. IANA . TORS . LOBE
IWONTKNOWANYTHINGINIT
NERDS . MITTS . NOON
RST . TULANE . PINTA . JOS
ITSMAKINGMEVERYSLEEPY
. OKED . MONACO . REIN
MOVIE . PTBOATS . GAZES
ACES . BARKAT . DUOS
WHATDIDIDOTHERPEOPLESAY
SOL . EDAMS . AFRAID . ILO
. ELEM . HAIFA . TABOR
WHATIDSAYISNTTHEISSUE
ROLE . MEDS . ALPS
OLE . SAMOSA . PSSST . IONA
NEXTWEEKSLOOKSTOUGHER
GUEVARA . IGOTIT . RANSOM
. PISTOL . ROOSTS . ORSONS
```

40. BREW HA-HA

```
AMOEBA . PCCLONE . ASSIZE
DENVER . ORDERED . GANDER
INTENT . PARFORTHECOORS
NTH . IDEES . TSO . INKBLOT
. EAGER . HMO . BEDE
KIRINCARPENTER . ARISTA
EGAD . OSMAN . RNA . SIRS
ELDER . END . BUSCHLEAGUE
POI . EAR . KEEN . EELIEST
SOONAS . APIG . AREAMAPS
. UGHTHATSGROLSCH .
. SIDEREAL . FRET . EISNER
SEMINAR . AMOR . LST . ODO
PABSTMASTER . PTA . YARDS
ATAT . PAL . STANK . LEIA
NODSAT . OLDERBUDWEISER
. POST . RIA . AANDP .
WAIKIKI . BIO . ROUND . OLE
AMSTELSTANDING . ZINNIA
SENECA . INGENUE . AVISOS
PROLES . ACADEME . SELENE
```

41. PLEDGE OF ALLEGIANCE

```
COHORTS . ORO . IZE . WHIFF
ARMOIRE . TUNASUB . HANOI
DROPPINGTHEBONE . ISSUE
. MOO . ROLLINGSTALL .
SHAR . MRED . NED . ATONED
PONEBEARER . REAIR . EDS
ERODED . MUS . ALETA
ADDIN . HEIRTOTHETHRALL
REEDITED . RBI . THEBLUE
. TARES . OARS . OLLA
ALLFORONEANDONEFORALL
LEIA . SING . SAPAN
INERTIA . NAM . REALLOTS
TONEINTHESADDLE . YACHT
. SCENE . NOI . SIFTER
MAE . SOEUR . HONEOFFAME
ARMIES . NEA . ROAM . SLEW
ICECREAMCALL . ARE
MARIO . GALLWITHTHEWIND
EDGES . ANIMATE . HONOREE
DEERE . REP . YEN . SWEETEN
```

42. CYBERCHUCKLES

```
MILKBAR . GENERA . ATTACK
ONLEAVE . ELUDER . MRBLUE
STODGES . LADYOFLEISURE
TOYS . EDDIES . INB . MSN
ETD . SALOONS . PAESE . NEO
LOSSOFLIFE . FAVA . CAIRN
. OHNO . SKIPABEAT .
ALFA . USAF . NEALON . OLDE
BILL . LABOROFLOVE . BOAS
STOIC . XEROX . NEMO . ARP
TINTED . KEVIN . YONDER
AND . OAFS . ICERS . HOSNI
ITOO . LAPOFLUXURY . TOOT
NONS . ISRAEL . TRIO . EFTS
. LOSTASTEP . YALL .
ANSON . BITE . LEGSOFLAMB
TOW . SWANS . WAVIEST . UAR
PSI . HAL . SHYEST . ANNA
LANDOFLINCOLN . SLOWDAY
ALGORE . LEASES . AUBERGE
YESTER . LATETO . TIEDYED
```

43. SMOOTH MOVE

```
A L A S K A ■ A M A D ■ B I K E ■ D A M
D E N I A L S ■ S A N I T A R I A ■ I T A
Z I O N I S T ■ E Y E S O C K E T ■ M E T
■ S T O N ■ M O T H E R ■ C A L I
S F C ■ H O L B ? ■ I R T ■ D A P H N I S
A I R M E N ■ C I T A D E L ■ N I E C E S
T R I C K ■ S T E R ■ E R A ■ O C H R E
W E E ? ■ L I V ■ E U R ■ S T L U K E S
E D D ■ F O X ■ ? A N ■ T H E I S M
L O O ? A T ■ C A T H E R I N E ■ A M F
L O U S Y ■ L O N E ■ D U N K ■ I T A L O
R T E ■ F O U N D L I N G ■ I C E R U N
N A D I N E ■ B B ? ■ D O H ■ ? I E
V A G R A N T ■ C O L ■ P A N ■ W A D S
P A U L I ■ E D O ■ E B A Y ■ R E M I T
U N T I E D ■ M I N D S E T ■ P E S E T A
B L O S S O M ■ A C E ■ ? H E A D ■ S Y R
G I S H ■ C O A L E R S ■ S A Y B ?
A N E ■ S I L V E R M A ? ■ S P O I L E D
M E A ■ A L T E R N A T E ■ T A N N E R Y
E S T ■ M E S S ■ S L E D ■ L E G R E E
```

44. WHAT A PICTURE IS WORTH

```
I C I N E S S ■ C C I N G ■ H I J A C K
M A D I S O N ■ F O L D E R ■ A M E C H E
B R I T T L E ■ A M E L I A ■ M O T R I N
R O O S E V E L T ■ V E N N ■ I N T E R N
U L M ■ E S T A T E ■ S T O L I ■ A P E
E S S A Y ■ G H A L I ■ O T T ■ G E D
■ R U B L E ■ S A N ■ A Z O ■ V E R Y
F R A N K L I N ■ T N T ■ B E N J I
E O S ■ S U E ■ F E D O R A ■ O A S T S
S O S O ■ I D L E S ■ W A S H I N G T O N
S K I P ■ S T O W ■ D E A N ■ R O L E
E I S E N H O W E R ■ C O R N S ■ A L T A
S E I N E ■ T R O J A N ■ G E T ■ E E K
■ T E M P O ■ D E F ■ C U R R E N C Y
J A T O ■ C A P ■ E F T ■ A P T E R
A N O ■ S K I ■ O F A L L ■ F I N A L
C N N ■ T I N C T ■ E N A M E L ■ E R E
K E E P O N ■ H O A R ■ S A C A G A W E A
S T R O L L ■ A I M S A T ■ O V E R T O N
O T O O L E ■ S T O O L S ■ L I N C O L N
N E W L E Y ■ E Y I N G ■ I N T O N E S
```

45. OVERHEARD DOWN UNDER

```
A M O R E ■ B U S ■ J A M B S ■ B A B A
J U D A S ■ M U S H ■ E C L A T ■ E M U S
U N E M P L O Y M E N T R I T E ■ Y O R K
G I R D ■ E X E C R A T E ■ M E M O I R S
■ O F A I R ■ R P I ■ M A R I N
O L D W I V E S T I L E ■ A N E C D O T E
D I O N N E ■ R E E S E S ■ D A T E R S
E G G ■ I N C L A S S ■ P T A ■ S H I E S
S H I P ■ S H O D ■ D I E G O ■ E L K E
S T E R E ■ E V E N S O ■ R E L A P
A S S I S I ■ E D A S N E R ■ D E I S T S
■ N E V E R ■ G R A T I S ■ F L E S H
O P E C ■ E S S E S ■ C C E D ■ E N T R
H I V E S ■ A L F ■ S N E E Z E R ■ S R I
O N I O N S ■ I T S H O T ■ A E G E A N
H A L F O P E N ■ C O N C O R D G R I P E
■ W O R S E ■ A O L ■ P I E T A
H A S I D I C ■ P R I E S T L Y ■ N O A M
U R A L ■ N O T H I N G L I K E A D I M E
B I L E ■ G R I E F ■ A O N E ■ L E N I N
S A K S ■ S T O N Y ■ L E G ■ I R K E D
```

46. THE ART OF THE DEAL

```
T A T E ■ D O S S I E R ■ A C C T S
B R E N T ■ A R I A N N A ■ S A G U A R O
S T R A I G H T F L U S H ■ P I E R S O N
P U R C E L L ■ T O T H ■ F I D E L I T Y
■ R A T S O ■ R E N E E ■ I C E S I N
■ S U R G E D ■ R A N E E S ■ C O P S
S C I ■ P I U S ■ T O T E R S ■ C U G A T
T A C H ■ A M E B A ■ H O C ■ O L E A R Y
A R E I ■ S P E A K ■ E N E S C O ■ M I N
10 J Q K A ■ D E T ■ R S T U ■ E S E
■ T S E ■ ♥ ♥ ♥ ♥ ♥ ■ R O D
M I R ■ O W N S ■ S R I ■ 9 10 J Q K
E D O ■ N E S T L E ■ A E S O P ■ A S I S
E L Y S E E ■ R E X ■ T R E V I ■ D U D E
S E A T S ■ S A N T E E ■ L A N A ■ P A T
E R L E ■ E T U D E S ■ A L L E G E
■ F A B L E S ■ M C A T S ■ F A R G O
C O L L E G E S ■ P A T H ■ S O T H E R E
A B U T T A L ■ T O P P O K E R H A N D S
F I S H E R S ■ D R E A M O N ■ A R I E S
E T H Y L ■ S E E R E S S ■ D I R E
```

47. IN PAIRS

```
D I M I T R I ■ B L U E S T ■ E M T
E X E D O U T ■ A E N E I D ■ J A I L E R
I N T E R N S I N T U R N S ■ E L N I N O
C A R S ■ A R A B ■ A T A C O S T
E Y E ■ I N H A L E I N H A I L ■ I T A S
■ M A I ■ N E A R M I S S
D E V I A N T S ■ K N A V E S ■ T E S L A
O R I N G S ■ O L E A T E S ■ L E S I O N
S I S Q O ■ F R O N T O N ■ S E V I L L E
E S A U ■ C R E A T E ■ S O N I N L A W
■ I N R O A D S I N R H O D E S
P O T R O A S T ■ N O H I T S ■ I L E S
A M H E R S T ■ T E E T E R S ■ E Z I N E
S I R I U S ■ A R T I S T E ■ O R E L S E
S T U N S ■ E R I N G O ■ S O N G S T E R
■ C H A N U K A H ■ N E O
D I S H ■ I N G E S T I N J E S T ■ C I A
I N H O U S E ■ N E A T ■ M E N U
O N E I L L ■ I N S I D E R I N C I D E R
D E A R M E ■ M O R B I D ■ M I A S A R A
E R R ■ P R I M E S ■ E X P E R T S
```

48. I CAN SEE WHY

```
F A T S O ■ T A R P ■ S E A L ■ S E R F
A M O O N ■ K A R E L ■ E L B A ■ O T O E
D I L L Y P I C K L E ■ W I N D Y F A L L
E L I X I R ■ S A N J O S E ■ A T I L T
■ T E P I D ■ C A E N ■ G I S E L E
A B A S E ■ R U E R S ■ E A T I N
L I R R ■ T R E N D Y S E T T E R ■ D E R
P L A Y A ■ H A I ■ A H E M ■ D O L E
S S N ■ S H O R T Y W A V E ■ S C O W L S
■ D E L A N Y ■ E E L E R S ■ E N N I O
P A Y R A T E ■ N I L ■ H O N E Y E D
A N N A N ■ S U B T L E ■ C A R T E L
C O A S T S ■ B U L L Y D O Z E R ■ O F F
E S M E ■ I G O R ■ A L A ■ O C A L A
S E E ■ B E L L Y B O T T O M S ■ A D E N
■ B E G A T ■ A L I E N ■ C O P S E
S C A L E D ■ C L E M ■ S C A R S
E L E N A ■ D E A D S E T ■ A B A T E S
B U L K Y H E A D ■ T O A D Y S T O O L S
B R I E ■ I N R E ■ R U F U S ■ E N N U I
S P A R ■ P S S T ■ A T T N ■ D E S E X
```

49. LABORATORY MAZE

```
R O S T R A   N R A   F L O J O   T A R P
O R A T E D   S E L F R A T E D   O M O O
D E M O D E   F O L L O W O N E S N O S E
E L O P I N G   I S M   L E E R A T
N S A   G O O V E R T H E W A L L
T E N D   V I R U S   N A T   A C L U
    E S S   S A D I E   S T A R C H E S
G E T C A U G H T I N A M O U S E T R A P
D U R A T I O N   G E L   T W A I N S
A R A L   O U I   H E A D D R E S S
Y O N   W E S   S T A R T   R A T   T A R
    S T R E E T A R T   S O Y   P I T A
A P P E A R   I I I   P E A C E N I K
G R O W T I R E D O F T H E R A T R A C E
F O R E H E A D   S L A I N   A R E
A M T S   N Y U   A R T I S   C I R C
    M A K E S A T E S T R U N   N E H
T O P J O B   A B C   I T E R A T E
B A R E L Y S Q U E A K B Y   T E E P E E
S H A W   S U B S T R A T A   E D S E L S
P U T S   M E S A S   Y U M   R A T T L E
```

50. TWO, PLEASE

```
B O A T   O C T   F U C H S   A S H L E Y
U N U S A B L E   A S H E N   R O M E R O
S C R A N T O N   R O O M A N D B O A R D
H E A R T A N D S O U L   C E E   P O E
      I E O H   R O C K A N D R O L L
H E R E A N D N O W   S O O T   O O F
U T I C A   S O H O   N N E   S O F I A
M C C A L L S   E P P S   R O S T A N D
S H O R T A N D S W E E T   C E S I U M
    T O B O O T   C A R A C A S   T R I
B A L E   R O M A N   R U N O N   W H E T
L E I   C A T E R E R   E N R A G E
A T T H A T   B R E A D A N D W A T E R
I N T E N S E   O D I N   S A Y N O T O
R A L L Y   C P A   D E P P   N E S T S
    E G O   H E R R   W A I T A N D S E E
L A W A N D O R D E R   I C E D
E M O   E E K   B A L L A N D C H A I N
T I M E A N D S P A C E   R U S H I N T O
I G E T I T   U R G E S   O R I E N T E D
N O N A M E   P O S S E   S E N   D I M E
```

51. GETTING PERSONAL

```
M A B   A D I D A S   C I R C E   I S T
I C E   G E N E S I S   S N O O T   G E O
C T S   R A G I N G H E A D W A I T E R S
H A T T E R   A N O N   E X C I T E S
E L L I E   A P P E A L E D   K L I N E
L O A N   A I R   T A X I S H E L T E R
I N I T   A D O R N   R E S H O T
N E D   T H E G O I N G S H O W   S C A T
    P R E S   O G E E   E S C U D O
A B L E R   A R M E E   E R A   L A T E R
P E A C E   M A I L D E M E R   A T T A R
P L I E S   A G E   I L E F T   T H O L E
L A N D A U   U N I T   F E E T
E S S E   S E E I N G S I T A R S   H R S
    S E T T L E   E C O L E   P E E K
H I S A N D H E I R S   W E T   A C M E
A N I T A   S E E T H I N G   N I H I L
S C R U F F S   C O O T   B O R A T E
T H E B U I C K S T O P S H E R E   I T T
E E N   E X A L T   L I T E R A L   S E A
D D S   D E M M E   N O N E T S   E E L
```

52. WHO SAID IT?

```
T A K E S F I V E   P A D S   W A R T S
E V E N M O N E Y   A L I A S   O S H E A
T E D T U R N E R   S T E P H E N K I N G
E R S E   S E P T E T   E N T E N T E
    R I D I   R A R I T A N   D O H S
S H E   F I N I T O   E N U R E
C A L V I N C O O L I D G E   A R C H E R
A D M I T   U L E E S   A D E L I N E
D I E S   R A T   H E D D A   D E L T A
S T R A D A   N O M   G E R A L D F O R D
    O D E T T E   O P I A T E
A N D Y W A R H O L   N E V   D R A F T S
M A S O N   R E E D S   N E O   M A R C
I P C R E S S   K U D O S   L O V E R
D E S E R T   A N N A K O U R N I K O V A
    R O M E O   A N T I C S   R I P
A B A B   A C C U S E S   C O T Y
P O L E N T A   T H R E A D   A M M O
S O P H I A L O R E N   M A R K T W A I N
E T H A N   A T A R I   I N T E R L A C E
S H A N E   E L S E   S E E R E S S E S
```

53. SCIENTIFIC AMERICAN

```
A G T   I R A S   T A C T   T S A R I S T S
P O H L   N E U T   A G A R   H A M O N R Y E
A R E A   S A T E   K A R O   A V A I L I N G
C O O P   P R I N C E T O N   T A T   A S E A
H U R T   I V S   A H E M   L E G I T
E N Y O   T I M B R E   S T A V E   H A D A T
A D O P T E E   U S A F   E V E L   E B O L A
N S F   H O W   T O R O   A E R Y   N I E L S
    R E E F S   E N T R   F R Y   N O T S O
N U E V O   A N S   T A O   T R I B   N R A
A R L E N   I L E   I R R   H O N E   T N N
I S A   L I M B   E = M C 2   I T A L   H O N
V A T   Y O R E   U T E   R N S   P L A N A
E M I   R U E R   G O I   S E G   R I P E N
    I V I E S   T S E   S P A T   C H I M P
A N I M A   W E A N   S I L O   R O Z   E S C
C O T E S   E I R E   O T I S   O N E I N C H
T R Y T O   A N G S T   B E S S I E   C A R A
    N U R S E   A M O R   A S S   E T A S
M O C S   B A T   P H Y S I C I S T   M O N T
A N A E R O B E   L I E S   A L A I   A N T I
M I N N E L L I   E T R E   P O N E   N C O S
O N E T O T E N   D I S S   A N T S   E N E
```

2009 *International Holidays*

Following are the dates of major holidays in 2009 for selected countries. Islamic observances are subject to adjustment. Holidays of the United States, United Kingdom, and Canada, and major Jewish holidays, appear on this calendar's grid pages. Pomegranate is not responsible for errors or omissions in this list. Users of this information should confirm dates with local sources before making international travel or business plans.

Please note: Most international holidays that fall on a weekend are observed on the following Monday (or the next working day).

ARGENTINA
1 Jan	New Year's Day
24 Mar	National Day of Memory for Truth and Justice
2 Apr	Veterans Day (Malvinas War Memorial)
9 Apr	Holy Thursday
10 Apr	Good Friday
12 Apr	Easter
1 May	Labor Day
25 May	Revolution Day
20 Jun	Flag Day*
9 Jul	Independence Day
17 Aug	San Martín Day*
12 Oct	Día de la Raza
8 Dec	Immaculate Conception
25 Dec	Christmas

* Observed on the third Monday of the month.

AUSTRALIA
1 Jan	New Year's Day
26 Jan	Australia Day
2 Mar	Labor Day (WA)
9 Mar	Labor Day (Vic)
	Eight Hours Day (Tas)
	Adelaide Cup (SA)
16 Mar	Canberra Day (ACT)
10–13 Apr	Easter Holiday
14 Apr	Easter Tuesday (Tas)
25 Apr	ANZAC Day
4 May	Labor Day (Qld)
	May Day (NT)
1 Jun	Foundation Day (WA)
8 Jun	Queen's Birthday (except WA)
	Volunteer's Day (SA)
3 Aug	Picnic Day (NT)
	Bank Holiday (NSW, ACT)
28 Sep	Queen's Birthday (WA)
5 Oct	Labor Day (NSW, ACT, SA)
3 Nov	Melbourne Cup (ACT)
25 Dec	Christmas
26 Dec	Boxing Day
28 Dec	Proclamation Day (SA)*

* Observed on the first weekday following the Christmas public holiday.

BRAZIL
1 Jan	New Year's Day
20 Jan	São Sebastião Day (Rio de Janeiro)
25 Jan	São Paulo Anniversary (São Paulo)
23–24 Feb	Carnival
25 Feb	Ash Wednesday (morning only)
10 Apr	Good Friday
12 Apr	Easter
21 Apr	Tiradentes Day
1 May	Labor Day
11 Jun	Corpus Christi
7 Sep	Independence Day
12 Oct	Our Lady of Aparecida

2 Nov	All Souls' Day
15 Nov	Proclamation of the Republic
20 Nov	Zumbi dos Palmares Day (Rio de Janeiro, São Paulo)
25 Dec	Christmas
31 Dec	New Year's Eve Bank Holiday

CHINA (SEE ALSO HONG KONG)
1 Jan	New Year's Day
26 Jan	Chinese New Year Holiday begins
1 Feb	Last day of New Year Holiday
1–7 May	Labor Day Holiday
1–7 Oct	National Day Holiday

FRANCE
1 Jan	New Year's Day
12 Apr	Easter
13 Apr	Easter Monday
1 May	Labor Day
8 May	Victory Day (WWII)
21 May	Ascension Day
31 May	Pentecost
1 Jun	Whitmonday
14 Jul	Bastille Day
15 Aug	Assumption Day
1 Nov	All Saints' Day
11 Nov	Armistice Day (WWI)
25 Dec	Christmas

GERMANY
1 Jan	New Year's Day
10 Apr	Good Friday
12 Apr	Easter
13 Apr	Easter Monday
1 May	Labor Day
21 May	Ascension Day
31 May	Pentecost
1 Jun	Whitmonday
3 Oct	Unity Day
25 Dec	Christmas
26 Dec	St. Stephen's Day

HONG KONG
1 Jan	New Year's Day
26–28 Jan	Spring Festival / Lunar New Year
5 Apr	Grave Sweeping Festival
10–13 Apr	Easter Holiday
1 May	Labor Day
2 May	Buddha's Birthday
28 May	Dragon Boat Festival
1 Jul	Special Administrative Region Establishment Day
1 Oct	National Day
5 Oct	Mid-Autumn Festival
26 Oct	Chung Yeung Festival
25 Dec	Christmas
26 Dec	Boxing Day

INDIA
1 Jan	New Year's Day
14 Jan	Makar Sankranti

26 Jan	Republic Day
9 Mar	Prophet Muhammad's Birthday
11 Mar	Holi
3 Apr	Rama Navami
7 Apr	Mahavir Jayanthi
10 Apr	Good Friday
12 Apr	Easter
9 May	Buddha Purnima
15 Aug	Independence Day
20 Sep	Ramzan Id (Eid-al-Fitr)
26–28 Sep	Dussehra
2 Oct	Mahatma Gandhi's Birthday
17 Oct	Diwali (Deepavali)
2 Nov	Guru Nanak's Birthday
27–29 Nov	Bakr-Id (Eid-al-Adha)
18 Dec	Muharram (Islamic New Year)
25 Dec	Christmas

IRELAND
1 Jan	New Year's Day
17 Mar	St. Patrick's Day
10 Apr	Good Friday
12 Apr	Easter
13 Apr	Easter Monday
4 May	May Holiday
1 Jun	June Holiday
3 Aug	August Holiday
26 Oct	October Holiday
25 Dec	Christmas
26 Dec	St. Stephen's Day

ISRAEL
10 Mar	Purim
9 Apr	First day of Pesach
15 Apr	Last day of Pesach
21 Apr	Holocaust Memorial Day
28 Apr	National Memorial Day
29 Apr	Independence Day
29 May	Shavuot
30 Jul	Tisha B'Av
19–20 Sep	Rosh Hashanah
28 Sep	Yom Kippur
3 Oct	First day of Sukkot
10 Oct	Shemini Atzeret/Simhat Torah

ITALY
1 Jan	New Year's Day
6 Jan	Epiphany
12 Apr	Easter
13 Apr	Easter Monday
25 Apr	Liberation Day
1 May	Labor Day
2 Jun	Republic Day
29 Jun	Sts. Peter and Paul (Rome)
15 Aug	Assumption Day
1 Nov	All Saints' Day
8 Dec	Immaculate Conception
25 Dec	Christmas
26 Dec	St. Stephen's Day

JAPAN

1	Jan	New Year's Day
12	Jan	Coming of Age Day
11	Feb	National Foundation Day
20	Mar	Vernal Equinox Holiday
29	Apr	Showa Day
3	May	Constitution Memorial Day
4	May	Greenery Day
5	May	Children's Day
20	Jul	Marine Day
21	Sep	Respect for the Aged Day
22–23	Sep	Autumnal Equinox Holiday
12	Oct	Health and Sports Day
3	Nov	Culture Day
23	Nov	Labor Thanksgiving Day
23	Dec	Emperor's Birthday

MEXICO

1	Jan	New Year's Day
5	Feb	Constitution Day*
21	Mar	Benito Juárez Day†
9	Apr	Holy Thursday
10	Apr	Good Friday
11	Apr	Holy Saturday
12	Apr	Easter
1	May	Labor Day
5	May	Battle of Puebla (Cinco de Mayo)
16	Sep	Independence Day
1	Nov	All Saints Day
2	Nov	All Souls Day (Day of the Dead)
20	Nov	Revolution Day†
12	Dec	Our Lady of Guadalupe
25	Dec	Christmas

* Observed on the first Monday of the month.
† Observed on the third Monday of the month.

NETHERLANDS

1	Jan	New Year's Day
10	Apr	Good Friday
12	Apr	Easter
13	Apr	Easter Monday
30	Apr	Queen's Birthday
4	May	Remembrance Day
5	May	Liberation Day
21	May	Ascension Day
31	May	Pentecost
1	Jun	Whitmonday
25–26	Dec	Christmas Holiday

NEW ZEALAND

1–2	Jan	New Year's Holiday
22	Jan	Provincial Anniversary (Wellington)*
29	Jan	Provincial Anniversary (Auckland)*
6	Feb	Waitangi Day
10	Apr	Good Friday
12	Apr	Easter
13	Apr	Easter Monday
25	Apr	ANZAC Day
1	Jun	Queen's Birthday
26	Oct	Labor Day
13	Nov	Provincial Anniversary (Canterbury)*
25	Dec	Christmas
26	Dec	Boxing Day

* Observed on the closest Monday.

PUERTO RICO

6	Jan	Three Kings Day (Epiphany)
11	Jan	Eugenio María de Hostos Day*
22	Mar	Emancipation Day
10	Apr	Good Friday
12	Apr	Easter
16	Apr	José de Diego Day†
17	Jul	Luis Muñoz Rivera Day†
25	Jul	Constitution Day
27	Jul	José Celso Barbosa Day
12	Oct	Día de la Raza
19	Nov	Discovery of Puerto Rico
24	Dec	Christmas Eve

All US federal holidays also observed.
* Observed on the second Monday of the month.
† Observed on the third Monday of the month.

RUSSIA

1–6	Jan	New Year's Holiday
7	Jan	Orthodox Christmas
23	Feb	Defender of the Motherland Day
9	Mar	International Women's Day
19	Apr	Orthodox Easter
1	May	Spring and Labor Day
11	May	Victory Day
12	Jun	Independence Day
4	Nov	National Unity Day

SINGAPORE

1	Jan	New Year's Day
26–27	Jan	Chinese New Year Holiday
10	Apr	Good Friday
12	Apr	Easter
1	May	Labor Day
9	May	Vesak Day (Buddha's Birthday)
9	Aug	National Day
22	Aug	Beginning of Ramadan
20	Sep	Hari Raya Puasa (Eid-al-Fitr)
17	Oct	Deepavali
27	Nov	Hari Raya Haji (Eid-al-Adha)
25	Dec	Christmas

SOUTH AFRICA

1	Jan	New Year's Day
21	Mar	Human Rights Day
10	Apr	Good Friday
12	Apr	Easter
13	Apr	Family Day
27	Apr	Freedom Day
1	May	Worker's Day
16	Jun	Youth Day
9	Aug	National Women's Day
24	Sep	Heritage Day
16	Dec	Day of Reconciliation
25	Dec	Christmas
26	Dec	Day of Goodwill

SOUTH KOREA

1	Jan	New Year's Day
25–27	Jan	Lunar New Year Holiday
1	Mar	Independence Movement Day
2	May	Birth of Buddha
5	May	Children's Day
6	Jun	Memorial Day
15	Aug	Independence Day
2–4	Oct	Harvest Moon Festival
3	Oct	National Foundation Day
25	Dec	Christmas

SPAIN

1	Jan	New Year's Day
6	Jan	Epiphany
9	Apr	Holy Thursday (Madrid)
10	Apr	Good Friday
12	Apr	Easter
1	May	Labor Day
15	Aug	Assumption Day
12	Oct	National Day
1	Nov	All Saints' Day
6	Dec	Constitution Day
8	Dec	Immaculate Conception
25	Dec	Christmas

SWEDEN

1	Jan	New Year's Day
5	Jan	Epiphany Eve
6	Jan	Epiphany
9	Apr	Maundy Thursday
10	Apr	Good Friday
12	Apr	Easter
13	Apr	Easter Monday
30	Apr	Walpurgis Eve
		King's Birthday
1	May	May Day
20	May	Day Before Ascension
21	May	Ascension Day
31	May	Pentecost
6	Jun	National Day
19	Jun	Midsummer Eve
20	Jun	Midsummer Day
30	Oct	All Saints' Eve
31	Oct	All Saints' Day
24	Dec	Christmas Eve
25	Dec	Christmas
26	Dec	Boxing Day
31	Dec	New Year's Eve

SWITZERLAND

1	Jan	New Year's Day
10	Apr	Good Friday
12	Apr	Easter
13	Apr	Easter Monday
21	May	Ascension Day
31	May	Pentecost
1	Jun	Whitmonday
1	Aug	National Day
25	Dec	Christmas

THAILAND

1	Jan	New Year's Day
9	Feb	Makha Bucha Day
6	Apr	Chakri Day
13–15	Apr	Songkran (Thai New Year)
1	May	Labor Day
5	May	Coronation Day
8	May	Visakha Bucha Day (Buddha's Birthday)
7	Jul	Asanha Bucha Day
8	Jul	Khao Phansa (Buddhist Lent begins)
12	Aug	Queen's Birthday
23	Oct	Chulalongkorn Day
2	Nov	Loy Kratong
5	Dec	King's Birthday
10	Dec	Constitution Day
31	Dec	New Year's Eve

2010

JANUARY

s	m	t	w	t	f	s
					1	2
3	4	5	6	7	8	9
10	11	12	13	14	15	16
17	18	19	20	21	22	23
24/31	25	26	27	28	29	30

FEBRUARY

s	m	t	w	t	f	s
	1	2	3	4	5	6
7	8	9	10	11	12	13
14	15	16	17	18	19	20
21	22	23	24	25	26	27
28						

MARCH

s	m	t	w	t	f	s
	1	2	3	4	5	6
7	8	9	10	11	12	13
14	15	16	17	18	19	20
21	22	23	24	25	26	27
28	29	30	31			

APRIL

s	m	t	w	t	f	s
				1	2	3
4	5	6	7	8	9	10
11	12	13	14	15	16	17
18	19	20	21	22	23	24
25	26	27	28	29	30	

MAY

s	m	t	w	t	f	s
						1
2	3	4	5	6	7	8
9	10	11	12	13	14	15
16	17	18	19	20	21	22
23/30	24/31	25	26	27	28	29

JUNE

s	m	t	w	t	f	s
		1	2	3	4	5
6	7	8	9	10	11	12
13	14	15	16	17	18	19
20	21	22	23	24	25	26
27	28	29	30			

2010

JULY

s	m	t	w	t	f	s
				1	2	3
4	5	6	7	8	9	10
11	12	13	14	15	16	17
18	19	20	21	22	23	24
25	26	27	28	29	30	31

AUGUST

s	m	t	w	t	f	s
1	2	3	4	5	6	7
8	9	10	11	12	13	14
15	16	17	18	19	20	21
22	23	24	25	26	27	28
29	30	31				

SEPTEMBER

s	m	t	w	t	f	s
			1	2	3	4
5	6	7	8	9	10	11
12	13	14	15	16	17	18
19	20	21	22	23	24	25
26	27	28	29	30		

OCTOBER

s	m	t	w	t	f	s
					1	2
3	4	5	6	7	8	9
10	11	12	13	14	15	16
17	18	19	20	21	22	23
$^{24}/_{31}$	25	26	27	28	29	30

NOVEMBER

s	m	t	w	t	f	s
	1	2	3	4	5	6
7	8	9	10	11	12	13
14	15	16	17	18	19	20
21	22	23	24	25	26	27
28	29	30				

DECEMBER

s	m	t	w	t	f	s
			1	2	3	4
5	6	7	8	9	10	11
12	13	14	15	16	17	18
19	20	21	22	23	24	25
26	27	28	29	30	31	

Personal Information

name _____

address _____

city _____ state _____ · zip _____

phone _____

cell/pgr _____ fax _____

e-mail _____

in case of emergency, please notify:

name _____

address _____

city _____ state _____ zip _____

phone _____

physician's name _____

physician's phone _____

health insurance company _____

plan number _____

allergies _____

other _____

driver's license number _____

car insurance company _____

policy number _____